New Methods of Market Research and Analysis

G. Scott Erickson

Professor of Marketing, School of Business, Ithaca College, USA

Cheltenham, UK • Northampton, MA, USA

Published by
Edward Elgar Publishing Limited
The Lypiatts
15 Lansdown Road
Cheltenham
Glos GL50 2JA
UK

Edward Elgar Publishing, Inc.
William Pratt House
9 Dewey Court
Northampton
Massachusetts 01060
USA

Paperback edition 2019

A catalogue record for this book
is available from the British Library

Library of Congress Control Number: 2017941907

This book is available electronically in the **Elgar**online
Business subject collection
DOI 10.4337/9781786432698

Printed on elemental chlorine free (ECF)
recycled paper containing 30% Post-Consumer Waste

ISBN 978 1 78643 268 1 (cased)
ISBN 978 1 78643 269 8 (eBook)
ISBN 978 1 78990 105 4 (paperback)

Typeset by Servis Filmsetting Ltd, Stockport, Cheshire
Printed and bound in the USA

Contents

Figures

Tables

Prologue

Some years ago, at a meeting with the Advisory Council for our School of Business, a senior executive from Bausch & Lomb strongly encouraged us to rename our Marketing Research course. His suggestion was to change it to Marketing Analytics, based on what was happening in his industry and others he had observed. We had a sense of the dramatic changes starting to occur and immediately followed his recommendation even though we weren't entirely sure about what to do with it.

The challenge then was to figure out how to actually alter the course beyond the name. My research stream, for many years, focused on intangible assets of the firm, including not only formal patents and such but also harder to define knowledge, intelligence and data. The research has always focused on real activities at real firms, so the beginnings of widespread interest in big data and business intelligence were hard to ignore. Many of the sources of big data were found in marketing and compelling applications were starting to arise that were of interest in the course. The proposed merger of Omnicom and Publicis in 2013, for example, was sold as a means of building the scale to do the necessary data analytics required in digital advertising. Even though the deal fell apart, the reasoning behind it held. If even a creative, qualitative industry like advertising was heading in the big data/marketing analytics direction, it seemed inevitable that it would affect everyone at some point.

Around the same time, one of our top recent alumni came back to campus to recruit and present to students. She had been working for Nielsen for a few years. Her talk with students illustrated what Nielsen would do in evaluating a market opportunity for a proposed new offering in a consumer good category. She walked through an environmental analysis, a competitive analysis, and metrics on consumer behavior in the product category. What was interesting was that not one piece of data came from communicating with consumers, from a traditional focus group or survey or something similar. Everything was based on data Nielsen had already collected. From market size to market shares, from consumer buying preferences to their reactions to price-offs, everything came from internal Nielsen databases or external data to which they had access.

In a traditional marketing research course, much of the emphasis is on communication techniques, particularly questionnaires. Moreover, a lot of related material revolves around questionnaires, including instrument design, administration, sampling, and even things like coding and data entry. And a lot of courses require student projects, almost invariably an assignment to create, administer and report the results from a survey. One can't imagine marketing research without techniques like focus groups and surveys; they'll always be an important part of our toolset. But one can imagine a different emphasis more in line with contemporary practice.

Marketing analytics suggests that different emphasis, utilizing all the information resources available to a firm in order to explore marketing-related questions. As the course developed over time, I began to watch more carefully what was happening at firms doing interesting things with big data in a marketing context. I developed a number of case examples for use in class as well as some exercises focused more directly on understanding data and what to do with it. One issue, however, was that marketing research texts didn't seem to change much during this time. Some new details were added such as the use of mobile devices for administration or the possibility of virtual focus groups. But, invariably, these were short tack-ons to main sections and didn't really reflect their growing importance. Marketing research texts still tended to center on communication-oriented research projects, especially surveys.

At the same time, statistical work in such texts generally included basics like means and standard deviations, where appropriate, as well as hypothesis testing, confidence intervals, and basic regression. All can be important but, again, the examples and any included exercises tended to flow from modest sample sizes and could easily be handled by standard Excel worksheets. So as I began incorporating big data concepts into courses, I found less and less of a match with what I was doing vs. available marketing research texts. More and more needed to be brought in from other sources.

In teaching marketing analytics, however, I also found increasing levels of math phobia in students. Part of that is that my own students aren't just from the Business School but also from a Communications School that cooperates with us on an Integrated Marketing Communications degree. Math skills seemed to be declining while, at the same time, the advanced techniques found in data manipulation and data mining were requiring even higher levels of proficiency. So the statistical work in research/analytics was becoming daunting, with a number of students expressing the feeling that they just "weren't good at math".

In talking to recent alumni and colleagues, however, and in learning more about big data and analytics, I found that the trends seemed to be in the direction of multifunctional teams. Those conducting the data analysis were often a marketer combined with a data scientist and a statistician. Even those directly involved in analytics weren't going to be conducting the analysis themselves. But they would need to know how to converse with the data scientists and the statisticians. Those not directly involved would be the consumers of the research. They just needed to understand the results they were given and enough about how they were generated to have a feel for what the data meant and what the limitations might be.

In several visits to SAS' training facility in Cary, NC, I acquired a sense for what analytics software could provide. But my most recent course, on SAS Visual Analytics, really opened the door to what I wanted to be able to do with students. The intuitive, drag-and-drop software was easy to use and generated a variety of visually appealing reports. This was the type of output I thought my students would be seeing, and generating it would acquaint them with advanced data monitoring and analysis techniques to which I thought they should be exposed. I soon incorporated SAS Visual Analytics into the course.

But after all these changes, I was left without a text that I thought presented what was really happening in terms of research design, data gathering, data analysis and data reporting. This book is an attempt to fill that hole. Although structured around a classic marketing research course framework, especially related to research designs, it covers many of the major trends in the field and focuses on what actual firms are doing with big data and marketing analytics.

In particular, the text highlights the explosion in observation research seen in data collected on web behavior, social media activities, transactions and their context, geo-location tracking, and similar advances. It also looks at the increase in combinations of observation and communication results, the ability of firms to track behavior and then ask subjects about the motivations and feelings behind it. The growth in ongoing relationships between firms and identifiable individual consumers is covered as an important trend, as is the variety of technologies available for gathering the data, including the internet and mobile apps. How researchers better motivate and engage subjects is included. And students are provided with details and hands-on illustrations of what the techniques for big data monitoring and predictive analytics actually look like, including the visualizations for reporting.

This book would probably best fit as a supplemental text in an under-graduate marketing research course, where students receive the traditional coverage but can also see the key advances over the last decade. But it has also been structured to stand by itself. Traditional topics are highlighted in each chapter, and students are well-versed in filling in the details by means of Google search, so it can be used as a stand-alone text if desired. It's written for advanced undergraduates or for more specialized gradu-ate courses (which might include more work with the software). The data analysis examples feature SAS Visual Analytics, which can be accessed at www.teradatauniversitynetwork.com but other advanced analytics soft-ware could be used instead.

My thanks go to the Ithaca College School of Business for granting me the sabbatical leave during which this book was written. Thanks also go to the Fulbright Program, particularly the Iceland Fulbright Commission, as a good amount of work on the book was done while at Akureyri University when I wasn't spending time sitting alongside the fjord. And thanks also to my IC marketing analytics students who have had the content tested on them over the last few years and responded to the challenge.

1

Big data and marketing analytics

Contemporary marketing research and analytics is considerably different from how research was conducted even as recently as a decade ago. A number of trends have driven these changes and will likely lead to even more drastic differences in the future. In order to fully understand data-driven marketing, one needs to understand the processes behind it. New professionals coming into the field should have a basis in both big data and analytical tools for examining that data. In order to do so, it helps to look at the context of these innovations and how they have matured over time.

BIRTH OF LOYALTY PROGRAMS #1

One of the earliest and most effective modern loyalty programs was created in the 1990s when UK retailer Tesco launched the Clubcard. Tesco employed marketing analytics provider dunnhumby to install the card-based system and later acquired the consumer science provider. The Clubcard loyalty system was set up not just to reward consumers but also to gather enough data to allow better understanding of the customer and then create closer relationships. At this time, when Walmart's low prices and convenient locations threatened to overrun less efficient retailers, Tesco and others saw customer knowledge as an alternative means to compete. With better knowledge, they could serve customer needs better and counter pure price appeals.

At its beginning the Clubcard was supported by information technology (IT) resources though these were fairly limited compared to today's capabilities. But they did allow for substantial data collection and subsequent analysis. Out of 50 000 or so items (stock-keeping units or SKUs), researchers were able to identify 10–12 000 key ones. These were assigned scores according to a few dozen identified characteristics. In one example, papayas might be characterized as high on "[a]dventurous, fresh, premium price, short shelf life".

Classification by characteristics allowed Tesco to analyze entire shopping baskets as it collected transaction data. Associations could be found between items shoppers tended to buy together, initially by hand but eventually by computer as algorithms were developed to spot frequently occurring buying patterns. Based on the similarities in the baskets, Tesco could identify customer segments. Deeper analysis of the shopping baskets and corresponding segments allowed researchers to form hypotheses about who might buy more, what promotional offers might spur purchase, and what non-grocery services might appeal to consumers (e.g. banking, telephone).

Tesco and dunnhumby further enhanced their transactional data and shopping basket descriptions with demographic (age/life stage) and behavioral (promotional responses, shopping time and location) detail. By 1994, according to one source, Tesco could offer 4 million different, distinct offers to consumers based on these variables. Though still based on segments as opposed to individuals (except for a few personal characteristics that could generate an offer), the numbers worked out to an almost one-to-one capability for the grocer's 10 million Clubcard members.

At this time, Tesco moved advertising dollars away from television and pursued a communication strategy heavy on direct mail and point-of-sale devices such as shelf-talkers. Members would receive quarterly mailings with an update on points, a newsletter, and targeted promotional offers. Additional mailings for special purposes were also made as well as communications aimed at sub-clubs (wine lovers, parents with new babies, etc.). Local stores could also be supported, especially when presented with special circumstances such as a new store opening by a competitor.

Note, again, that all of this was in the mid-1990s. IT was available, including early email capabilities, but not powerful in today's terms. Communication was chiefly done through mail. And the overall tactics were predicated on identifying and pursuing segments of customers.

Today, Tesco and dunnhumby are not as far ahead of the pack as was the case two decades ago but their capabilities have advanced considerably. dunnhumby serves multiple clients, not just Tesco, analyzing 5–75 terabytes per client; 700 million consumers are being studied, including 200 million weekly shopping baskets and 1.4 billion individual items. In addition, the agency combines shopper data with additional inputs such as weather, geography, demographics and social media. The data are structured and unstructured. Unstructured, though currently only 10 percent of the database is growing much more quickly, at 10–15 percent per year. dunnhumby notes one client in northern California, Raley's, using transaction and loyalty card data along with customer comments and social media chatter to target individual customers, improving their experience.

And that is probably the key take-away in terms of how big data and marketing analytics are changing practice in loyalty programs. Previously, loyalty programs were able to sort customers into segments, create offerings for segments, and push offers. Today, not only have organizations moved beyond mail as a principal means of communication, but they are able to identify and target individual customers by collecting all available data on behavior. Internal data are combined with other databases, again often identifiable down to the individual customer. From that understanding of each consumer, marketers can not only design promotional offers but actually enhance the relationship. Ideas for products offered on deal, types of communications, or other individual outreaches may still come from analyzing segments, but the actual marketing proposition can be made to distinct consumers.

dunnhumby sees the future of loyalty programs in those terms. As we'll discuss, big data and marketing analytics allow the collection, storage and processing of considerably more data than was the case even as recently as five years ago. As such, much more data on loyalty members can be created and stored, from a wide variety of sources. Combining profiles with other databases is also much more easily done. As dunnhumby client director Oliver Harrison points out, the point of loyalty programs is to identify customers (and one could add, identify the best customers, allowing appropriate approaches to every level of customer). But, in the future, rather than push marketing offers to customers based on profiles, loyalty programs will be designed to ease transactions and optimize the entire relationship. Instead of requiring loyalty cards, identification will be made by any number of technologies. Mobile apps, phones themselves and credit cards can all identify individual customers once tied to an account. Once identified, shopping activities can be tracked, including geo-location technologies with iBeacons that can monitor in-store movements. Background data, observed activities and contextual information can all be combined, stored and analyzed to allow real conversations with customers. Hearing each individual voice enables higher levels of customer satisfaction by making it easier for them to express desires and then fulfill them.

One of the key aspects of big data is this granular level of data collection and use. We'll talk about that in more detail as well as how analytical tools and capabilities can create even further insight. Big data is one of those terms that get thrown around a lot, but not everyone really understands what it means. This chapter should clarify the details as well as those surrounding related concepts such as analytics.

BIG DATA #1

So if big data is a ubiquitous and perhaps overused term, what exactly is it? One thing to note is that big data and marketing analytics (or marketing intelligence) are related concepts but not necessarily the same thing. In this section, we'll be looking at some aspects of the combination of big data and marketing analytics that apply chiefly to the former. The reasons should become clear but note that the terms are closely related but probably shouldn't be used interchangeably.

Big data is sometimes referred to as a dataset too big to be handled by traditional software tools (the phrase "too big for Excel" is sometimes used). That is somewhat imprecise, but even that has a purpose as processing and storage tools are expected to change, so the software programs will get more powerful but the databases are also likely to continue to grow. Further, big data differs by context. What might be considered big data in one industry would be considered a relatively small dataset in another. So, in some sense, we know big data when we see it but there is also a sense of not wanting to be pinned down in defining it.

But there are more precise descriptions that are helpful. In particular, big data is sometimes referred to according to the "three V's": volume, velocity and variety. Volume refers to the amount of data generated by various sources, fed into the system, and stored. McAfee and Brynjolfsson report that in 2012, 2.5 exabytes of data were created every day and that amount was doubling every three years or so. An exabyte is one billion gigabytes. We'll talk about sources shortly, but the bottom line is that the amount of data being generated and captured is exploding.

Velocity is the speed of the data collection and transfer. Quarterly reports on sales have been replaced with transactional data updated by the nanosecond. Retailers can track what is happening in stores in real time. Website operators of all kinds can do the same. Data are much more available than was previously possible. Variety has to do with the nature of the

Table 1.1 Useful terminology

Big Data	Volume	Gigabyte Terabyte Petabyte	1000 Megabytes (MB) 1000 Gigabytes 1000 Terabytes
	Velocity	Speed at which data enters, is processed, and exits system (e.g. annual, weekly, hourly, seconds, micro-seconds)	
	Variety	Structured	Ordered data, usually quantitative
		Unstructured	Unordered data, at least in raw form (e.g. text, images, video)
Enterprise Systems	Enterprise Resource Planning (ERP)	Information technology system for managing all resources of the firm's operations (inputs, processing equipment, human resources, etc.)	
	Supply Chain Management (SCM)	Information technology system for managing the firm's supply chain, ensuring right inputs arrive in right place at right time	
	Customer Relationship Management (CRM)	Information technology system for managing all interactions with individually identified customers (transactions, communications, etc.)	
Big Data Systems	Data Lakes	Combination of all databases of firm in one place, often requiring considerable work to rationalize different data systems and formats	
	Key Performance Indicators (KPIs)	Metrics identified as key to achieving performance objectives, monitored on a regular basis	
	Dashboards	Screens designed to report important metrics, often KPIs and often in a visual format appealing to the decision-maker	
Analytics	Deeper analysis using advanced tools capable of handling the volume and complexity of big data		

data inputs. Practitioners in the field often refer to structured (traditional, quantitative) vs. unstructured (not quantitative) data. The latter category includes all sorts of inputs that previously weren't stored in databases or, if stored, were very hard to organize and analyze. Today, unstructured data such as recorded voice, text, log files (such as machine performance or activity tracking), images and video are all regular parts of databases. Monitoring things like customer attitudes with video, call center comments, or social media chatter is both do-able and subject to analysis. Some key observers believe the ability to enter unstructured data into databases is *the* key piece of the big data concept, and it may be. But unstructured data usually takes up a huge amount of storage and processing capacity (volume) and is valuable, in part, because it can be monitored in real time (velocity), so all three V's do have a part in our understanding of the concept. Some observers add more V's to the definition, specifically veracity (truthfulness or accuracy) and value, which can have their place as well.

From where do all the data come? Firms installed enterprise systems in the late 1990s and into the new century. These included enterprise resource planning (ERP), supply chain management (SCM), and customer relationship management (CRM) systems. ERP has to do with tracking and bringing together everything needed for operations (raw materials and components, labor, machine availability, etc.) in the most efficient manner. SCM does much the same with inputs from suppliers, while CRM records all interactions with customers. These systems generate tremendous amounts of data, everything to do with supply chains, operations, distribution channels, vendors and consumers. Early generation installations created the data but it wasn't necessarily all tracked or stored after the fact. But one key reason for the advent of the big data phenomenon is the drop in costs of computing storage and processing. Firms can afford to collect and keep everything from all systems; they can also afford to distribute it more widely and/or subject it to deeper analysis.

This is part of why the cloud is an interesting part of the package. Cloud computing is nothing magical, it's just a matter of moving data storage and processing to third party systems. So organizations rent space on systems provided by Amazon, Microsoft, Google, or another provider, and that solution is cheaper than installing their own servers and such (as well as personnel needed to service them). Cloud computing is more an indicator of the tremendous drop in computing costs mentioned earlier.

With an affordable structure to take in and process ever more data, the door was opened to new sources of inputs as well. As noted, social media (text, images, video), customer comments (audio, text), and other data-heavy inputs that we've referred to as unstructured data also joined the party. The digital world that has developed over the past decade has substantially increased the amount of potentially relevant data for organizations, particularly for marketers.

All of that has to do with data internal to the organization or at least internal to it and its network of collaborators. But the trends propelling interest in big data have also created opportunities for firms to collect, store and process other sources of data, both publicly sourced (e.g. government, visible social media) and commercial. Not only does this add to the amount of data available to the system but enables combinations of data. The term "data lake" has come into the conversation recently, referring to the ability of firms to combine all kinds of databases into one huge, accessible collection. Harmonizing the databases into a single format in a data lake is no small task but, again, contemporary technology and reduced costs have enabled firms to do so.

What these capabilities allow from a marketing standpoint, in particular, is an ability to create even more detailed profiles of individuals within a database. So if an organization has records on an identifiable consumer, it can supplement those records with items from other sources. From government records, for example, voter registration, professional credentialing, and real estate transactions can be harvested. Commercial sources may have all sorts of data, in general or identifiable to an individual consumer, from online and offline activities (product and service registrations, social media profiles, or from a multitude of other communications and observations). All it takes is one connector between databases, such as an address, to join together even anonymized profiles. One Federal Trade Commission report asserts that a profile exists for virtually every consumer in the United States.

Once a profile exists, firms can add to it. In particular, transactions and communications can supplement what the organization knows about any individual customer, provided they can be identified by means of loyalty check-ins, mobile apps, registered credit cards, and other records already on file. Essentially, the technologies are there to allow firms like dunnhumby and its clients like Tesco to collect massive amounts of data. Affordable tools are also available to store, organize and analyze all of this data, and the end result is personalization on a level we couldn't even conceive just a decade ago. Where else that leads, we'll discuss shortly.

BIRTH OF LOYALTY PROGRAMS #2

A second well-known pioneer of loyalty programs is Caesar's (formerly Harrah's), the casino/resort operator. The firm introduced its Total Rewards loyalty program in 1997 (then called Total Gold). At that time, just about all casinos had some sort of rewards program, especially for the high rollers referred to as "whales". But Harrah's went further, seeking to do something about the legendary fickleness of customers (even loyalty members reportedly spent only 36 percent of gambling dollars at Harrah's at that time) by means of the greater geographical spread of its properties. The firm also found that the vast majority of its revenues came from gambling (over 87 percent in 2001) rather than hotel rooms, shows, stores or restaurants. Total Gold tracked demographics and transactional data from members, including gambling spending and preferences (cards were inserted in slot machines, for example, to earn points, and machines of choice could be tracked).

Total Rewards was installed to increase visits to Harrah's properties, thereby increasing loyalty. Looking more deeply into the existing database, managers found that 26 percent of customers generated 82 percent of revenue. Essentially, different customers had different value to the organization. Moreover, the most valuable ones weren't the whales but middle-aged and senior slot players, often current or former professionals. These customers didn't necessarily stay overnight, playing on trips home from work or on weekend outings and typically responded better to promotional offers centered on the gambling experience (free chips) than on other perks (room discounts, free meals).

The loyalty program evolved to include both more detailed descriptions of member preferences and an enhanced service capability to improve delivery on those preferences. Different information systems were linked together into a winner's information network (WINet) so that a single database included all available data, including transactions, gameplay, hotel management, reservations and background demographics. This database could be updated hourly at the time. Records were analyzed to determine long-term potential, the customer lifetime value. These data showed different customer groups with different values, and loyalty program levels were designed to match those groups. Rewards were established not just as rewards but as a means of increasing lifetime value. These were personalized to the individual, specific promotional offers for each member.

But the marketing proposition wouldn't work without service excellence, so the customer database was also linked back to the hospitality and management staff. Names were used by everyone from the valet to casino floor staff. Rooms were set up as guests desired. Members were steered to their preferred activities. And, again, the service level could vary by loyalty program level, with some guests experiencing virtually no line at check-in or at restaurants and others having a normal check-in experience. According to at least one manager, customers didn't have a problem with different treatment; they understood that in the gaming industry the highest value players warranted the best service.

Today the system has evolved to even higher capabilities. Even though Caesar's has had some rough years following the 2008 economic meltdown (a bad time to be highly leveraged as the entire gambling industry took a hit), its big data program is still highly respected. Customer information records were estimated to be worth $1 billion, the highest valued asset in Caesar's bankruptcy portfolio. The firm continues to collect all available data about member behavior. Loyalty cards, for example, are now loaded with funds, and when at a gambling station can be inserted and tracked. So not just networked slot machines, but all forms of gambling can be monitored, including time spent, wins and losses. Video images can track lines, especially for high-value individuals. If a particularly valuable member has a bad night, staff can intercept them before they leave the casino, providing a personal interaction and incentive to return.

So the emphasis on data and excellent service continues but the data have become even more granular. Membership incentives represent an even wider range of options, not just promotional offerings like free rooms or shows but pricing differences (reservation agents can price based on supply, demand, and the individual customer's data profile) and product differences (what's included in the reservation package). Mobiles have entered the equation, both as a data-gathering tool (location data, social media chatter) and as a service device (alerting members to show times, game availability and time-sensitive offers). Algorithms have also been installed so that the system automatically takes action to improve the customer experience when it senses something has gone off track. When a member with an established pattern (visit to a specific property once a month with $X spent) halts that pattern (no visit in three months or reduced spending per visit), customer service reps can be alerted to make an outreach with a specific offer.

The Caesar's example again illustrates the nature of big data, that deep and detailed data are available on individual customers. Those data can be monitored for established behaviors, and changes in trend can be spotted while time is still available to do something about them. Further, such actions can be "automated" with algorithms and other decision-making rules, providing prompts to customer service reps or even independently fixing a problem, making responses even more rapid. Finally, as we'll discuss, such rich databases can also be analyzed for even further insights, those that might not be apparent without a deeper dive into the data lake.

BIG DATA #2

So firms are taking in high volumes of data, of all types of variety, at increasing velocity. That's the input part of the big data equation. What do the organizations do with the data and what are the outputs? As noted repeatedly, one key feature of big data is the unstructured data coming into the firms. These types of data are converted into an analyzable form by various programs such as one known as Hadoop. Once in appropriate digital form and organized in a manner that can be accessed and manipulated in a number of ways, the data can be fed out and reported, subjected to deeper analysis, or used for modeling. This section chiefly focuses on the first: data monitored and reported on a regular basis or data harvested for a specific purpose.

If monitoring data is the primary purpose of a system, it is set up to take in the data, perhaps summarize it or reduce it to descriptive statistics, and then report it out to appropriate parties. This could take many forms. It might be transaction data, sales of specific products, for example, or sales by location at retail stores. It might be image or video data, as would be the case with Caesar's' attention to lines in its casinos. It might be log data, perhaps from the internet of things. GE, for example, is able to monitor the performance of its airplane engines in real time. When any of the key indicators moves out of tolerance, action can be taken to correct the problem.

When that is the case, the data system is set up only to process, store and distribute the data. As noted, summary statistics might be reported but no major transformations of the data take place. When the system is set up, decision-makers do need to settle on what data are important to track. Based on historical data, benchmarks or target levels of the indicators can be determined. These are typically referred to as key performance indicators (KPIs). Monitoring systems are established to feed the KPIs to decision-makers, who then make necessary adjustments if those KPIs are out of line. Typically, these will be at the operational (adjust the machinery, adjust how web pages load) or marketing (adjust customer communications, adjust the price) level.

To illustrate, Tesco, discussed earlier in this chapter, uses KPIs to monitor daily outcomes at individual stores. The "corporate steering wheel" tracks data related to customers, community, operations, people and finance. For the customer category, for example, the grocer's high-level objectives include:

- earn lifetime loyalty;
- aisles are clear;
- I can get what I want;
- the prices are good;
- I don't queue (stand in line);
- the staff are great.

At the store level, the related KPIs reported by managers, again for customers are:

- gaps on shelves (product outages);
- I don't queue;
- mystery shoppers.

These may be measured at different times. Managers might do an hourly sweep, for example, to look for empty shelves. Lines at cash registers could be watched by managers, again perhaps on an hourly basis. Or they could be monitored in real time by video cameras. Mystery shoppers might appear on a daily, weekly or monthly basis. And these KPIs are undoubtedly supplemented with the massive data Tesco generates on transactions. Cash registers can be monitored constantly concerning category or individual product sales, use of promotional offers, responses to price experiments, and other matters. But the main point is that systems are set up to constantly feed raw or summarized data to decision-makers. These data are often presented on "dashboards". Dashboards are set up to monitor and communicate pertinent data, typically KPIs, to decision-makers. As indicated by the term, they provide a quick look at current performance, just as a car dashboard lets you know immediately important indicators such as speed, RPM and temperature. In some cases, the dashboard may be set up to provide alerts as performance goes outside set limits (e.g. temperature gets too high). Embedded analytics may even contain an algorithm that prompts a remedial action without a direct action from the decision-maker (e.g. engine automatically corrects to bring temperature down).

In Tesco's case, this could involve some of the KPIs noted above, customer data from loyalty cards and transactions, or other real-time performance indicators. Dashboards might be set up, for example, to monitor and communicate data on hourly (or even minute-to-minute) sales, use of Clubcard offers, stock levels of key items and so on. If an item on offer gets below a certain safety stock level, the dashboard might alert a store manager. Or, if embedded analytics are programmed into the system, an order to a supplier or distribution center might be sent out automatically.

But, again, the key point is that some big data systems are set up in this way to collect, organize and distribute information to decision-makers in real time. These types of systems might do some basic processing of the data, such as converting it to summary statistics or tables/charts. Or they may just transmit the raw data to be viewed on dashboards. And all of this can be quite useful, improving operations and marketing processes, increasing efficiency, and reacting to events quickly, perhaps even before a problem occurs. But deeper analysis of the data is not necessary and not necessarily completed. Not everyone needs the more complex systems in order to benefit from big data, though some do.

SPOTIFY

Spotify is a firm using big data in some obvious ways as well as some not so obvious. The obvious part includes the capabilities we just discussed: gathering and distributing big data. The less obvious part has to do with deeper analysis and new insights, something that can't be accomplished with the data sharing systems in isolation.

By late 2015, Spotify had 75 million subscribers to its digital music service, some paid and some taking advantage of the free service. Their activity amounted to 1.7 billion hours of listening per month or around 20 billion hours per year. If you have an account, the service is able to track everything you listen to and has also accumulated data from your registration, from other web-tracking information, and, perhaps, Facebook if accounts are linked. From tracking behavior, Spotify is able to gather even more data, aiding its profile of you and on the music played, such as location, time and the full range and depth of musical interests. All told, this amounts to 4 terabytes of storage just for music files, 600 gigabytes of listening data added daily, and 28 petabytes of total storage. Spotify possesses one of the largest data warehouses in the world. In fact, given our earlier discussion about the economics of the cloud, it's not surprising that the service recently announced it would move its data storage and process-ing to Google Cloud.

Spotify's initial success came from copying pirating services, down to the level of replicating some of their software. From such peer-to-peer con-nections, in addition to a centralized streaming ability, Spotify sought to offer the quickest "click to sound" experience in music streaming (utiliz-ing the network of users and stored music rather than just a centralized storage location). Operational data helped to further optimize the listen-ing experience. Another point of differentiation was the playlist. While listeners could easily move across platforms to competitors, whether iTunes, other pay services, or pirate sites, the playlist was something that was a chore to replicate, once built. A listener taking the time to construct numerous playlists on Spotify would be less likely to move to a different provider.

Big data stores are clearly of help in providing an excellent listening expe-rience to subscribers. Categorizing music in numerous ways allowing easy search and identification, the operations are seamless, and listeners today are provided with their own personalized statistics on listening patterns. What is often not seen is the value provided to artists and labels.

With purchased music, whether CDs or digital rights such as iTunes, all the provider really knows is when and where the product was bought. Whether the customer listens once or hundreds of times is opaque unless some other tracking ability is available (e.g. a trackable app). With Spotify, when, where, how much, and context can all be discerned. This sort of data can be invaluable to musicians, publishers and live event planners. Greeley (2011) provides the example of Jay Z sales being very high in London, UK, but listening rates actually showed him to be more popular in Manchester. Similarly, by city, Spotify can identify who is being played on Friday and Saturday nights (at parties), what music spikes after being added to radio playlists or being featured on a television show, and what tracks or playlists are being shared with friends. This sort of data can drive more effective concert planning, promotional efforts and media appearances. Artists have a much better handle on where and with whom they are popular.

In fact, more recently, Spotify has introduced an artist service to identify "high passion" fans. Its own data indicate that such fans are five times more likely to attend shows, so such data is of even more use to artists than just the basic data. Further, such users, though only 10–20 percent of the fan population, contribute to the majority of the artist's sales (streaming revenues, in this case). Accumulating data on different types of usage helps to identify the high passion fans. Spotify can identify fans who have listened to an artist every day in the last week. It can identify fans who listen to an artist more than any other artist. And it can identify fans who have listened to an artist for the majority of days in the last month. Add it all up, and you have a pretty good idea of who your best customers might be if you are a musician. You also have a way to reach them, and a stream of constantly updated data allowing you to track these numbers and spot trends. How this fits into what we discussed earlier concerning dashboards and KPIs should be readily apparent.

But Spotify is also indicative of higher abilities of big data, the applications beyond just monitoring, sharing and informing that we've been discussing. With all that data, firms are capable of deeper analysis. There are various approaches to examining the data for unexpected insights, and we'll discuss them in this book, but collectively they make up what is referred to as marketing analytics or marketing intelligence. More broadly, outside the marketing context, these would be business analytics or business intelligence. In some cases, the approach may simply be "cutting" the data differently by introducing a different variable providing a different perspective. When data are sorted by an additional variable or two, they can sometimes provide a totally different insight. Or the approach may be advanced statistical analysis allowing researchers to spot patterns in the data. We'll discuss several of these in more detail.

In Spotify's case, the data analysis capabilities are substantial. In terms of cutting the data, context was mentioned earlier. Spotify Labs employs a program named Cassandra to analyze listening preferences. One example provided concerns a heavy metal fan according to general listening patterns. But the individual is a young married professional with young children, so heavy metal recommendations from Spotify in the evenings would not be appropriate. Context matters, and the deeper analysis provided by adding that variable alerts the firm to the need for better recommendations depending on time of day, listening device or other variables.

Discover Weekly is one of Spotify's newest products, a personalized weekly playlist of recommended songs. The songs tend to be new to the listener, as are most of the artists. The recommendation is based on a mix of the listening history of the individual, the listening history of other individuals with similar profiles, and linkages between songs and artists noticed across the Spotify database (again, especially for those with comparable profiles). All of this is aggregated into a brand new playlist every week for each customer.

Further, even if the customer doesn't like everything on the playlist, Spotify collects additional data every time they click on a song on the playlist, listen to more material from one of the included artists, or add a song or artist somewhere else in their collection of playlists. All of this constantly provides additional data for the listener's profile, allowing Spotify to learn and even better customize the experience. As noted earlier, this is very different from a big data system simply compiling and sharing out results. This is deeper analysis, looking for insights in the data, creating knowledge or intelligence rather than just the raw data or information. In the manner in which the system itself learns from new data, processes and acts, it's a form of artificial intelligence or machine learning. That's big data at a different level, more along the lines of marketing analytics.

MARKETING ANALYTICS

Deeper analysis of databases can be done in a number of ways. We'll cover some of the basic techniques when we look at some statistical software later in this text. For now, it's just a matter of having some sense of how marketing researchers can manipulate data to get answers to questions or to uncover new insights. So Tesco trying to describe the best customer groups for a new product offering such as banking services, or Spotify trying to predict what new music you might like, based on your listening habits and those of similar customers, are both examples of instances where the data needs to be processed in order to come up with answers.

At the most basic level, such processing might just be a matter of "cutting" the data differently, adding a variable to a tabulation and observing the results. One of the most famous examples of this approach has to do with fatal automobile accidents. If insurers could identify the highest risk groups and charge accordingly (they can't always as discrimination by some of these variables is illegal), their marketing mix could be much more effective. Consider the data in Table 1.2.

Table 1.2 Fatal passenger vehicle crash involvements, by gender, April 2001–March 2002

Male	Female
33 733	14 633

With no other inputs, one might reasonably conclude that females are safer drivers than males. But add some additional variables to the mix, and you get the results in Table 1.3.

By calculating in miles driven, one can immediately see that the differences between men and women aren't as dramatic as they seem. As opposed to twice as many fatal crashes (33 733/14 633 or 2.3:1), the ratio is only 2.5/1.7 or 1.47:1. Much of the explanation behind higher crash rates for males has to do with them driving more miles.

But when age is added in, the picture grows even more complex. The difference between males and females is much more pronounced at younger ages but totally disappears by the time both genders move toward retirement age. And if we just look at the age differences exclusive of genders, the dif-

Table 1.3   Fatal passenger vehicle crash involvements, by gender, mileage and age, April 2001–March 2002

		Male	Female	
16–19	Crashes	4257	1852	6109
	Miles	45 billion	35 billion	81 billion
	Rate (crash/ miles)	9.2	5.3	7.5
20–29	Crashes	8949	3172	12 122
	Miles	225 billion	156 billion	382 billion
	Rate	4.0	2.0	3.2
30–59	Crashes	15 027	6946	21 973
	Miles	845 billion	551 billion	1396 billion
	Rate	1.8	1.3	1.6
60–69	Crashes	2097	1008	3105
	Miles	128 billion	64 billion	193 billion
	Rate	1.6	1.6	1.6
70 and above	Crashes	3148	1571	4719
	Miles	76 billion	39 billion	116 billion
	Rate	4.1	4.0	4.1
Total	Crashes	33 733	14 633	48 638
	Miles	1324 billion	847 billion	2172 billion
	Rate	2.5	1.7	2.2

Source: National Highway Traffic Safety Institute via Quora (2012).

ferences between the youngest group of drivers (7.5 crashes/million miles) and those in middle age (1.6 crashes/million miles) are substantial. And if one looks at multiple variables, the widest apparent difference is between males 16–19 (4257 crashes, 9.2 crashes/million miles) and females 30–59, (6946 crashes but only 1.3 crashes/million miles). It should be clear that an insurance company looking to set auto rates based on risk profiles would want to charge those young males considerably more than the more mature females, if possible.

The problem illustrated is referred to as "omitted variable bias", where missing a key piece of data leads you to an incorrect conclusion. It's also the reason why one aspect of marketing analytics, particularly predictive analytics, is repeatedly adding new variables to the process. So rather than just cutting the data by gender, in this case you would also want to add miles driven and age. Further detail from the statistics would let you know that alcohol consumption, speed and seat belt use are also critical variables that you would want to introduce. Once added to the analysis, all provide critical new insights into how you divide the market into smaller and smaller segments in order to better understand it and provide it with insurance products. If the true high-risk individuals could be identified and charged appropriately, prices would go down for everyone else. Different product packages could also be created for different segments.

Another illustration of the omitted variable problem, also referred to as Simpson's Paradox, comes from a famous court case in the 1970s. The Visualizing Urban Data Idealab at the University of California, Berkeley has an interesting, interactive representation of the data (http://vudlab. com/simpsons/), which come from the university itself. The data show that the school had accepted 44 percent of male applicants into its graduate programs but only 35 percent of female applicants. The surface data prompted a sex discrimination suit.

A deeper look at the data, however, uncovered a "lurking variable", one that provided a very different perspective when introduced. The data were cut not only by gender but also by department. There were departments with relatively high acceptance rates (typically math, science, engineering, etc.) and those with relatively low acceptance rates (more humanities and related disciplines). Women applied in much higher percentages to the latter. So, as illustrated in the online example, even though their per-department acceptance rates were higher than or virtually identical to those of men, the overall acceptance rate was significantly lower. As investigators pointed out, sexism may be apparent but it came from factors pushing women into the disciplines with higher rejection rates and occurred long before anyone ever applied to Berkeley. The university was not at fault as the deeper analysis of the data showed no evidence of institutional discrimination.

Cutting the data to better understand circumstances and, for marketing in particular, customer segments that may be revealed can be a fairly simple process, as in these examples. But remember that when one is doing it with millions of items and dozens or even hundreds of variables, it's not necessarily as easy as creating cross-tabulation tables. When the process is intended for what we call predictive analytics, specific techniques appropriate to large data sets are employed. We'll talk about some of these in more detail later, but basic regression, decision trees, or even neural networks can be used to correlate and group variables that might predict a specific outcome (e.g. purchase).

Conceptually, these processes can be similar to cutting the data but also different in some ways. Again, the main point is identifying and aggregating the variables predicting an outcome. With such identification, marketers can target customer profiles that are most likely to react with a specific action (again, purchase, visit to a website, enrollment in a loyalty program, etc.). Further, if certain marketing initiatives can be correlated to that specific action, those can also be employed most effectively. Essentially, exploring the data in depth with predictive analytics can engender much more effective marketing, down to the individual customer.

Perhaps the most notorious example of predictive analytics involved retailer Target. Marketing decision-makers there approached one of the firm's statisticians, Andrew Pole, to help them identify expectant mothers. Research suggests that many things bought at a store like Target are habit purchases. If those habits include buying certain products elsewhere (e.g. groceries), they are hard to break, even if the consumer is a Target shopper otherwise and the store carries the same products. But research also shows that major life events can trigger new habits. Nothing says major life event like a first baby. Marketers were interested in identifying expecting mothers at the beginning of their second trimester, then giving them incentives to develop a habit of shopping at Target for everything they would need before and after the newborn's arrival.

Target has a sophisticated big data program, tracking all points of contact with customers indicated by a Guest ID number. Credit cards, website visits, and other identifiable interactions with customers are fed into the system and combined with other demographic and behavioral data, perhaps obtained externally from commercial suppliers. Pole started by looking at customers in the baby shower registry, identifying variables that might indicate a pregnancy. A common purchase like a natural body lotion or calcium supplement indicates little by itself but starts to point to pregnancy when combined with other variables. Eventually, 25 variables, when viewed together, were found to provide a fairly accurate "pregnancy prediction score". A hypothetical example provided in a *New York Times* article suggested that cocoa butter lotion, zinc and magnesium supplements, a purse large enough to also carry diapers, and a bright blue rug would generate a high probability that the buyer was about three months pregnant. In terms of what we were discussing earlier, Target was able to bring together these variables and use them to predict purchase behavior in a specifically defined segment, making a strong case for the power of predictive analytics. The results were accurate enough to result in at least one complaint from a father about his teenage daughter receiving promotional offers related to pregnancy. It turned out she was pregnant, and Target knew it before the father did.

One last major approach to marketing analytics is clustering. Again, this is conceptually similar to cutting data and to predictive analytics. In fact, there can be overlap, as we'll discuss. But the point is to use multiple variables to group subjects together that have similarities. In a particular dataset of shoppers, for example, you might have a substantial segment all in the range of 24–30 years of age, female, single, employed in service industries, college degree, urban, and income $35 000 – $50 000. Another substantial segment might all be 55–60, male, married, self-employed, some graduate study, suburban, and income >$80 000. Other descriptive data, behaviors and attitudes might be added to these descriptions, including how good a customer they might be. The point is that with big data you might find more and richer variables concerning who they are, enabling you to better understand differences between the segments and how to approach them.

Clustering is apparent in what Spotify does with its listener pool. The idea of identifying listeners with similar tastes in music is based on grouping them together when their playlists overlap. So if two customers both like Jason Isbell, Chris Stapleton and Rhiannon Giddens, they can be grouped together and studied for other similarities, as well as how they might be dissimilar compared to another group of customers. It's much more complex than that, of course, and might get into hundreds of artist preferences and contextual details in defining the clusters. But the concept is very simple.

As noted, clustering could be used for predictive analytics as well. If one of the variables is a choice of interest (if most of a cluster who like artists A, B and C also like artists X, Y and Z, then others who are only identified with A, B and C might also like the latter choices), the extension can easily be made. But it has other purposes as well, mainly the deeper understanding that comes with ever more precisely defining clusters by descriptive variables, attitudes, behaviors and other items.

One final point to make in this section is the ability of these large databases to take in new information, analyze it, and adjust descriptions, predictions or other outputs accordingly. In traditional statistics, this is referred to as Bayesian statistics, specifically the belief that knowledge about a true condition is based on a probability but that the probability could and should change as new data about the true condition become available. In more contemporary terms, big data and marketing analytics are able to take advantage of artificial intelligence and machine learning. The analytical processes are able to learn from successes and failures. If predictions are right, that is incorporated into future predictions. The same thing is done if predictions are wrong. The waves of data provided by these big data systems enable continuous learning and real-time adjustments in analysis to take place.

BLOOMBERG

Bloomberg, owner of *Businessweek* magazine, a cable business news network and, perhaps most importantly, the ubiquitous Bloomberg terminals used throughout financial services industries, is a pre-eminent digital/ big data player. The firm generates 1.3 billion data points per day from its various digital properties. Some of this is available to advertising clients, clients generating tons of data themselves (though not always used effectively, generating opportunities for Bloomberg's operation).

In 2015 Bloomberg launched an offering called B:Match. The aim is to work with advertisers using its media outlets to identify appropriate target customers, add other available data to profiles, and then use the profiles to drive the media plan, tailoring messages and media to specific target profiles. As Bloomberg explains, its strategy is the opposite of Facebook. Instead of a single point of contact for virtually everyone, Bloomberg provides multiple points of contact for a very select group of consumers: affluent businesspeople. This group is in great demand for advertisers, not only for business-oriented products they might buy in their job-related roles but also for luxury or high-end products they might buy for their personal lives.

The purpose of Bloomberg, whatever the medium, is to inform its consumer base. Even before digital video became commonplace, the provider was comfortable with it, given its various distribution options (television, online as a supplement to the magazine, and online independently). It had the experience and talent to supplement and combine all the various outlets, adding to the experience of customers. Essentially, it can provide the information in whatever format customers desire. Consequently, it has a substantial and loyal customer base of affluent business professionals. And most of them are registered or otherwise identifiable by Bloomberg. Their business media consumption habits are trackable, by person, and can be supplemented with other data, often from external sources. Bloomberg typically has deep and detailed records of its customers.

Bloomberg has developed a number of initiatives to try to take advantage of its customer base, its knowledge of its customer base (big data), and what it can do with that knowledge, especially regarding advertisers. Advertising, of course, is its principal revenue source, so development of the database is essentially a means to make advertisers happy. B:Match is designed to find appropriate individual targets, flesh out their descriptions, and then help clients tailor their media plans to reach them. Context could also be supplied, including variables such as time of day and favored medium (for that time).

Examples provided include an unnamed airplane manufacturer that could use B:Match to identify Bloomberg users who might be customers, allowing them to track visits and activity at various Bloomberg sites. The advertiser could monitor topics in which they might have an interest (e.g. oil prices), observe the target individuals' activities on sites related to these topics, and then quantify interest in various advertising outreaches. Similarly, an advertiser seeking individual investors was able to identify them via Bloomberg's data on use of home computers to visit properties and tracking data showing previous stops at Yahoo Finance. Again, further data could be added to the descriptions once they were identified.

What can be done with the data and profiles once acquired? One client was targeting young, individual investors with display advertising (e.g. banner ads). With B:Match, they were able to identify targets, fill out descriptions, and then start to collect even more data on reactions to different ad choices. Choices such as optimal times of day, what types of content best complemented the ads, and even creative matters like color palette could be determined from the resulting database. KPIs for the advertising rose 200–400 percent after optimizing these and other variables.

B:Match is also easily matched with other Bloomberg offerings for advertisers. Social Connect 2.0 allows segmentation according to the social media platform from which the user was drawn to the Bloomberg site. Trendr provides a way for advertisers to "buy in" to a trending story widget, tracking user behavior from when they first noticed the topic through their access of the story and subsequent behavior. Finally, Bloomberg Denizen offers advertisers a platform from which to use the media company's data to create infographics or other branded content to be run as "native advertising", sponsored content that looks similar to regular editorial pieces at the outlet (though explicitly identified as sponsored advertising). Insurance provider Zurich, for example, created 40 pieces of content with Bloomberg's help, including articles, infographics and video, that could be run across media platforms (online, print, etc.). Data were also provided to Zurich that helped with targeted specific pieces according to user profiles and behavior, social media trends and other variables.

Bloomberg Media is an example of a number of the practices described in this chapter. On one level, it constantly takes in data on use of its sites, apps and other content outlets. This is wide-ranging data, including background on users, their behavior while engaged with Bloomberg, and additional data from external sources. As noted, 1.3 billion additional data points every day meets just about anyone's definition of big data. These data can be collected and shared, as with the big data systems we discussed, evaluated against key performance indicators set by Bloomberg itself (media circulation and ratings, website traffic, app usage, Google Analytics) or by its advertisers (views, click-throughs, or other actions by targets). The data can also be analyzed for further insights and/or adjusted according to algorithms. If a particular piece of advertising is getting better results than others given certain situational variables, the system might automatically adjust to run it more in those circumstances and less in other circumstances. And, as noted, Bloomberg and its advertisers can analyze data and results to predict responses, such as users fitting a specific profile will click on a specific piece of native advertising or will respond more positively to a banner ad in a certain shade of red. Application of just about any big data or business analytics technique covered in this ad should be seen as potentially applicable to what Bloomberg and its advertisers are doing.

SUMMARY

This chapter has provided background on the concepts we refer to as big data and marketing analytics. As suggested by the structure of the chapter, these can be two different phenomena though they are also complementary and effective when used together. With an understanding of how big data works, you are more prepared to see how it affects marketing research and decision-making. Similarly, some exposure to analytics techniques prepares you for some of the advanced data processing you'll see in practice in upcoming chapters.

The key points to note are the wide range of inputs now available for data coming into organizations; how such data are organized, stored and shared; and then how the data might be analyzed. On a regular basis, data are coming into organizations related to all customer touchpoints. In the real world, registered or self-reported demographics, psychographics and other lifestyle data, shopper transactions (cash register data), geo-location data (where they are and have been), customer comments (live or by phone or web) and multiple other trackable interactions are readily available and freely surrendered by consumers. In the virtual world, web browsing patterns, app use, social media, customer comments or contacts (email or social media) and, again, any number of other trackable interactions are also available. These data can be traditional quantitative inputs, collected and stored in digital format. Or they can be unstructured data such as images, videos, text or other such inputs that can now also be reduced to a digital format and catalogued for sharing or analysis.

Modern technology allows all of these forms of data to be collected and stored in real time. Again, big data is about volume (lots of data), variety (in different forms) and velocity (coming in on an increasingly frequent basis). Retailers and service providers such as Tesco and Caesar's monitor an increasing number of data inputs from their physical facilities, tracking activity in multiple ways (admission to locations and events; digital connections to machines, cameras, checkout) as it happens. Virtual service providers like Spotify can constantly monitor not only customer music choices but also matters like context (time of day, type of device, location). As can Bloomberg, accumulating all kinds of data from its variety of web properties regarding customer activities (news, up-to-the-minute financial information, video, click-throughs) and preferences (site, device, format). All of this can be gathered, transmitted, categorized and kept because of the plummeting costs of storing and processing data, especially in the cloud.

From a big data standpoint, all of these inputs could be monitored and probably are. But the most important data are designated as key performance indicators and delivered to decision-makers, probably on specially designed dashboards. These dashboards present the data in whatever manner is desired, perhaps raw data, perhaps tabulated or cross-tabulated, or even in visual formats such as charts, graphs or gauges. KPIs are chosen by the organization to reflect its priorities. We've already discussed a number of Tesco's KPIs as well as some key indicators tracked by Caesar's, such as the length of lines or heavy losses taken by designated priority customers. Similarly, Spotify can track highest played songs, activity in specific locations, device trends and other matters. Bloomberg can track content popularity, content format, click-throughs, device choices and similar activities of interest. And the data requests/dashboard visualizations can be changed as priorities change. Again, it is up to strategists and decision-makers to specify the data they want to see on an ongoing basis.

Researchers will also be asked to look more deeply into the data. Sometimes this will be for a specific project, looking for a specific answer to some question. Sometimes it will just be investigation with no particular objective, just mining the data to see what can be found that could be interesting. Analysts can do this by cutting the data in different ways, by different variables to see what distinctions might be apparent in the results. Spotify can do this by slicing data sets into ever smaller groups, perhaps by location or musical genre. At a very specific level, it could even do so by particular artists or songs. Once you've separated Drake from Meek Mill listeners or Apple from Samsung users in Helsinki, you can delve into all the other variables to see what differences there might be (demographics, location, lifestyle, app usage and so forth).

Alternatively, analysts can conduct predictive studies, studying groupings of variables to see which are associated with some outcome of interest. Or clusters of variables might be identified that merit further examination even without a clear current objective. Bloomberg can find variables identifying decision-makers in energy or the airline industries. Their news preferences, including topics viewed, or choice of metrics to be regularly streamed across their devices could indicate such segments. These variables might also indicate a receptiveness to targeted advertising, including some of the new communication offerings discussed earlier. Longer views of online ads, click-through rates or other metrics might be connected to such designated segments. An ad targeted to the airline industry may generate better outcomes when shown to micro segments identified by behavior on Bloomberg properties and related demographics (from registration or combined with other data from other sources).

We'll talk about all of these things as we move through the book, providing details and context. Again, the main objective is for you, as a marketer, to have a good understanding of what big data and analytics have to offer. You can see the outcomes, from successful applications, combined with enough background on the underlying data management and analytical processes to understand how practitioners got there. We'll start with the different research designs employed in traditional marketing research.

BIBLIOGRAPHY

Brown, B., D. Court and T. McGuire (2014), "Views from the front lines of the data-analytics revolution", *McKinsey Quarterly*, March, pp. 1–8.

Brown, M. and K. Mishra (2015), "Personalization at Spotify using Cassandra", 9 January, available at https://labs.spotify.com/2015/01/09/personalization-at-spotify-using-cassandra/, accessed 30 October 2016.

Davenport, T.H. (2013), "Analytics 3.0", *Harvard Business Review*, December, pp. 65–72.

Davenport, T.H. and J. Dyche (2013), *Big Data in Big Companies*, May, International Institute for Analytics, available at http://www.sas.com/resources/asset/Big-Data-in-Big-Companies.pdf, accessed 20 October 2016.

Duhigg, C. (2012), "How companies learn your secrets", *The New York Times Magazine*, 16 February, online edition.

Federal Trade Commission (2014), *Data Brokers: A Call for Transparency and Accountability*, March, available at https://www.ftc.gov/system/files/documents/reports/data-brokers-call-transparency-accountability-report-federal-trade-commission-may-2014/140527databrokerreport.pdf, accessed 30 October 2016.

Gill, P.J. (2015), "Building customer loyalty", *Oracle Magazine*, March/April, online edition.

Greeley, B. (2011), "Daniel Ek's Spotify: Music's last best hope", *Businessweek*, 13 July, online edition.

Harrison, O. (2015), "The future of loyalty programs", available at https://www.dunnhumby.com/future-loyalty-programmes, accessed 30 October 2016.

Karolefski, J. (2015), "Accepting the big data challenge: Grocers need to step up to stay competitive", *Progressive Grocer*, 5 July, online edition.

Langham, M. (2015), "Spotify, big data, and the future of music streaming", *dottedmusic blog*, 21 November, available at http://dottedmusic.com/2015/music-industry/spotify-big-data-and-the-future-of-music-streaming/, accessed 30 October 2016.

Lehe, L. and V. Powell (2016), *Simpson's Paradox*, available at http://vudlab.com/simpsons/, accessed 30 October 2016.

Levinson, M. (2001), "Harrah's knows what you did last night", *CIO*, 6 June, available at http://www.cio.com.au/article/44514/harrah_knows_what_did_last_night/, accessed 30 October 2016.

Loveman, G.W. (2003), "Diamonds in the data mine", *Harvard Business Review*, May, online edition.

Manyika, J., M. Chui, B. Brown, J. Bughin, R. Dobbs, C. Roxburgh and A.H. Byers (2011), *Big Data: The Next Frontier for Innovation, Competition and Productivity*, McKinsey Global Services, available at http://www.mckinsey.com/ business-functions/digital-mckinsey/our-insights/big-data-the-next-frontier-for-innovation, accessed 30 October 2016.

Marks, J. (2016), "Spotify, big data, and the next generation of digital publishing solutions", 2 August, available at https://www.vearsa.com/next-generation-digital-publishing-solutions/, accessed 30 October 2016.

Marr, B. (2009), "Delivering success: How Tesco is managing, measuring and maximizing its performance", Advanced Performance Institute, available at http://www.ap-institute.com/media/4312/delivering_success_tesco.pdf, accessed 30 October 2016.

McAfee, A. and E. Brynjolfsson (2012), "Big data: The management revolution", *Harvard Business Review*, October, pp. 61–8.

McAlone, N. (2016), "Spotify has a clever plan to make more money from 'super-fans'", *Business Insider*, 3 April, online edition.

Moses, L. (2014), "Bloomberg gives its native ads a data spin", *Digiday*, 23 May, available at http://digiday.com/publishers/bloomberg-gives-native-ads-data-spin/, accessed 30 October 2016.

Moses, L. (2015), "Inside Bloomberg LP's big data play", *Digiday*, 15 January, available at http://digiday.com/publishers/inside-bloomberg-lps-big-data-play/, accessed 30 October 2016.

Quora (2012), "Why are women stereotyped as being worse drivers?", available at https://www.quora.com/Why-are-women-stereotyped-as-being-worse-drivers, accessed 30 October 2016.

Shannon, J. (2015), "What Bloomberg EMEA launched at the IAB Digital Upfronts", *Campaign*, 22 October, available at http://www.campaignlive.co.uk/ article/1369358/bloomberg-emea-launched-iab-digital-upfronts, accessed 30 October 2016.

Sluis, S. (2016), "One audience, all media: Bloomberg Media's biz-focused strategy", *AdExchanger*, 1 June, available at https://adexchanger.com/the-sell-sider/one-audience-media-bloomberg-medias-biz-focused-strategy/, accessed 30 November 2016.

Spethman, B. (2004), "Loyalty's royalty", *Chief Marketer*, March, pp. 32–41.

Spotify (2015), "Introducing Spotify Fan Insights", 17 November, available at https://artists.spotify.com/blog/introducing-spotify-fan-insights, accessed 30 October 2016.

Welch, M. and G. Westerman (2013), "Caesar's entertainment: Digitally personalizing the customer experience", 25 April, Capgemini Consulting/MIT Center for Digital Business, available at http://ebooks.capgemini-consulting.com/dm/ Caesars.pdf, accessed 30 October 2016.

2

Exploratory research design

Even though a major theme of this book is the ascendancy of huge amounts of data and our ability to analyze them, the changes taking place in marketing research over the past decade go beyond those obvious examples. Technological and analytical improvements have impacted all of marketing research, including methods that are principally qualitative. Changes in exploratory research have been as dramatic as some of the changes in more quantitative designs. Moreover, the trends behind what has happened in exploratory research design have much to do with those driving big data and marketing analytics more broadly.

ReD ASSOCIATES

Take, for example, ReD. ReD Associates is a Danish consultancy with offices in both Copenhagen and New York. The firm has received considerable attention in recent years for its unique approach to research and analytics as well as the results it has delivered for some high-profile clients. ReD has also been in the forefront of advocating a deep, qualitative approach to understanding what really goes on with customers and potential customers.

In particular, ReD employs anthropologists and other analysts with social science backgrounds, allowing them to take an in-depth, insightful dive into client issues and questions. ReD was part of an important insight for Lego into the complexity of its product offerings. The toy firm had responded to the threat from immediately satisfying video games with simple sets and electronics that had little to do with construction and much to do with other tie-ins (e.g. pop culture). The assumption was that overscheduled kids had little time to devote to Lego's more traditional immersive products. What ReD found in studying the market more fully was a dual desire in children. Yes, they liked the quick satisfaction of video games and similar things. But they also liked activities requiring some time to master. In particular, children gravitated to activities requiring skill development resulting in an observable outcome, an outcome they could demonstrate and show off to others. Consequently, Lego rethought its products and moved into more challenging building sets that have done very well in the market. It returned to Lego being Lego.

Similarly, ReD helped Samsung learn about television buyers often being less concerned with technical specifications than with how the device fits as a piece of furniture, appearance and design winning out over performance. Relatedly, they found out that television purchase decisions are more often than not made by females. ReD showed Coloplast that inexperienced ostomy bag users in real-life conditions had a very different challenge than healthcare professionals attaching bags in clinics. Once again, the result was an important product improvement.

What do they do? ReD is the epitome of a qualitative, exploratory research design firm, performing in-depth, open-ended studies with relatively small samples. Their purpose is often to uncover unexpected results and insights. In that way, it is fairly typical of a qualitative research operation. But some differences also exist, demonstrating how new analytics capabilities are affecting even exploratory techniques.

The process laid out in a *Harvard Business Review* article written by ReD's principals includes:

- Thinking differently about the research problem. Often this means taking a closer look at how consumers experience the product.
- Collecting data. Immersive or ethnographic studies are not new but the ability to record observations and communications and store them, at least to do so in large quantities, is. Researchers insert themselves into the lives of targeted consumers, observing (and perhaps discussing) everything they do in relation to the product, including environment and interactions with others.
- Analyzing data. ReD famously has its PhD social scientists study the data for patterns, so a critical human element definitely exists. But the firm also uses analytical software to dig through the open-ended, unstructured data (including video) and categorize, aiding the more ad hoc review.
- Uncovering key insights. The end result should include a better understanding of how the client can improve user experiences.

Some of ReD's best-known work has been with shoe and sportswear maker Adidas. Several projects have been completed, all with the objective of obtaining a deeper understanding of target customers. In order to learn more about sportswear consumers, ReD trained Adidas product designers in ethnography, having them spend 24 hours with selected consumers. All activities, from meals to workouts, were to be done together. The specific point was to isolate what made them exercise, a factor that could impact sportswear purchases. Relatedly, another researcher conducted a projective study, mailing disposable cameras to women, asking them to photograph images that made them want to exercise. Twenty-five out of 30 cameras came back with pictures of little black dresses. From the in-depth results, researchers concluded that consumers weren't training for expertise at a sport but rather for general fitness and appearance. High performance mattered less than regularly participating in an activity.

For the London Olympics in 2012, Adidas was given the contract to outfit the home UK Olympic team. Again, ReD helped with the project, conducting research on what images the British associated with patriotism. The normal images that others think of as representing the UK (palace guards, double-decker buses) didn't resonate with the home community. Rather, more general images such as the national flag worked better, and uniform designer Stella McCartney was asked to think "untraditionally British". The result was the commercially successful uniforms featuring bits of the flag, but blown up so big as to be almost unrecognizable. A similar effort in Russia for 2014 World Cup uniforms pushed designers toward pre-1970 associations rather than something more contemporary.

ReD illustrates a number of the progressions in exploratory, qualitative research we'll be discussing in this chapter. From immersion in subjects' lives through ethnographic research to projective prompts, from deep probing questioning based on continuing contact to using contemporary technology to fully capture all behaviors, communication and context, ReD is an excellent example of forward thinking in qualitative environments. The firm is also at the forefront of analysis, having recently signed a deal allowing tech firm Cognizant to take an ownership stake. The blend of digital capabilities and deep qualitative approaches should open up even newer opportunities to push the envelope on exploratory research designs.

EXPLORATORY RESEARCH DESIGN

In a traditional marketing research course, you learn about exploratory research techniques used in securing qualitative, in-depth information from a small sample. The point is to gain a preliminary understanding of a decision-making environment, perhaps helping to develop hypotheses or appropriate courses of action. Unexpected answers are common. When the researcher doesn't know what the full range of responses might be, leaving the options open to participants makes sense. Exploratory research, like all research, can use observation or communication.

Table 2.1   Useful terminology

Data Type	Secondary	Data that already exists, not collected for the purpose of a research study
	Primary	Data collected specifically for a research study
Observation	Studies collecting data from observing behavior	
	Human/ mechanical	Refers to observer, whether it is a human watching and recording behavior or a machine collecting data on the behavior (e.g. web-trackers, transactions, facial tracking)
	Natural/ contrived	Refers to whether observation takes place in a natural setting (real world) or contrived/ artificial setting (such as a lab facility set up to look like a retail store)
Communication	Studies collecting data from communicating with subjects	
	Depth interviews	Structured conversations with individuals or groups
	Focus groups	Structured small group conversations with a moderator but also emphasizing group dynamics and cross-talk
Other Approaches	Ethnography	Observational study of the subject in their environment, may include communication as well. Immersion also inserts the researcher into that environment.
	Projective techniques	Vague stimulus designed to elicit unfiltered reaction from respondent. Can be used with observation or communicating.

Existing or secondary data or reports of both types may also exist. Especially with today's data storage capabilities, researchers should conduct a search to see if relevant information already exists before running off to do a new study. Archived interviews or focus groups, customer observations, customer comments, social media chatter are all possible sources of existing qualitative information. External providers may also already have in-depth studies of matters such as the buying process, customer likes and dislikes, media habits and so on.

Typical observation methods include:

- shopper tracking (paths consumers take within stores);
- mystery shopping (agent acts as if shopping and reports back on experience);
- audits (e.g. pantry contents, refrigerator contents, closet contents);
- content analysis (analyzing text for content, meaning, patterns);
- one-way mirror observations (often done to see reaction to new products);
- web paths (click patterns of individuals);
- social media postings (can be a form of content analysis).

Typical communication methods include depth interviews and focus groups. Ethnographic or immersive studies can have elements of both observation and communication and are indicative of an increasing number of studies that include both approaches.

Depth interviews can be done face-to-face or through telephone, mobile, internet or other technologies. They are often long (two hours or more is common, but almost always longer than a survey) and, though they usually have a structure to the questioning, are open-ended, allowing probing and the possibility of going off in unanticipated directions. They can allow demonstration, either handling of physical products or media (e.g. video, software or games). Group interviews have gained some interest in recent years, bringing down the cost of the tool and instilling a more social environment.

Focus groups are more than group interviews; they do bring together a small group (6–12) of people to interview but are structured to stimulate a group discussion. Note that the "focus groups" you sometimes see on television, especially related to politics, having someone wandering around an audience of 50–100 people with a microphone, aren't real focus groups. The moderators should not be having only a one-way conversation with individuals. The key to a focus group is the group dynamic that develops. There should be considerable cross-talk between participants. The moderator should keep to some structure but, again, the value is in the open-endedness, probing questions, and the way the participants themselves spark interesting comments from each other. Like depth interviews, focus groups can demonstrate products or concepts and an opportunity to observe non-verbal signals when done in person. That being said, focus groups are also seeing some trends toward online administration, though some group cohesion can be lost in virtual environments.

Ethnographic research involves studying people in their natural environment, particularly when interacting with a product. Immersion refers to situations in which the researchers insert themselves into that environment in order to perform the study. These overlapping techniques are particularly effective when the targeted consumer group is significantly different from the marketers themselves, so there is limited understanding of lifestyles and priorities. MTV, for example, is well-known for its decades-long commitment to ethnographic studies of its teenager and young adult market. Not only are executives at the company not part of that demographic but the cohort also changes over every few years. So today's teenagers are very different from those that were around when MTV launched in the early 1980s, and MTV needs to keep up with those changes if it is to change its programming to fit the new audience. Much of what ReD does is ethnographic and immersive work, such as the Adidas study on how and why individuals work out.

Projective techniques can be used with any of the tools just covered. Projection is the response to a vague stimulus that reveals true feelings about something. So instead of just asking whether a respondent likes something, you provide a seemingly unrelated task that reveals liking or not. The well-known Rorschach ink-blot tests are a projective technique as are standard marketing research tools such as sentence completion, role-playing and consumer drawings. As noted, projective techniques could be used in interviews, focus groups, or even ethnographic studies or observations when giving the subject something puzzling to which to respond. ReD's study with the little black dresses is an example of a projective approach, with the camera as the vague stimulus and the photos the open-ended feedback.

The advantages of an exploratory approach include depth and open-ended responses, resulting in the unexpected outcomes mentioned earlier, an ability to probe for further information, and an ability to further explore feelings and motivations. Exploratory research is flexible, usually has a reasonable total cost, and can be validated by further, more quantitative research.

The disadvantages of an exploratory approach are an inability to generalize from the results (what is true for one person or a small sample is not necessarily true for an entire population), the time needed to carry out such in-depth studies, the high cost per response, and the frequent need for highly skilled interviewers, observers and/or analysts. Essentially, you spend time and money getting to know a lot about some individuals but you don't study enough to make the results reliable for a wider group.

WHAT'S NEW #1?

So what's new in the area of exploratory research in the age of big data and analytics? Although the initial reaction might be that big data has little in common with qualitative research, and there are those in the field who agonize over either/or decisions involving the choice, the environment that allows lots of data and advanced analytics actually has its impact on qualitative research as well. And there is a place for both modern qualitative and quantitative approaches; researchers just need to know what each is good at and when to employ them.

To illustrate, consider some examples.

SKIM

SKIM, a London-based decision behavior-focused research firm, reported on a study its staff performed concerning the drug-prescribing behavior of physicians. The nature of the work involved Kahneman's System 1 (emotional, intuitive) and System 2 (rational, logical) theory for which he won a Nobel Prize. The basis of the theory is that people make decisions differently; they might be logical or they might be emotional (or a mix of both), something that marketers need to understand if they are to appeal to them. Subjects might respond better to marketers reasoning with them. Or they may be more receptive to marketers seeking an emotional response. Or both. The theory is often used in testing responses to advertising which emphasize logic or emphasize emotional impact.

In this case, the research question revolved around how oncologists prescribe cancer treatments. The thought was that a rational (System 2) choice evolves with time and repetition into a more emotional (System 1) choice, similar to how a consumer develops a brand preference. But to establish that insight and determine the circumstances surrounding the process, researchers needed to talk with doctors about prescribing behavior. Moreover, we know that emotional choices often have a short life, so asking the physicians to recall the process after the fact could be difficult and might lead to erroneous memories.

Consequently, researchers sought to catch physicians "in the moment" immediately after writing the prescription. To do so, they created a mobile app. In using it, physicians could quickly (less than five minutes) and easily submit their thoughts while fresh, ideally in between patients. The app included an open-ended function with which oncologists could describe by voice memo the reasoning behind their recommendation and also enter some close-ended data concerning the patient. The open-ended reporting was structured, with respondents asked to comment on "clinical history of the patient; summarize what was discussed during consultation; list treatments considered by the respondent during consultation; identify treatment chosen and reasons why; and provide reasons for not choosing any of the other treatments".

At the end of the study, the researchers had accumulated 500 responses, very large for an exploratory study. The analysis revealed a rational element, that recommendations were based on the patient's circumstances and intended outcomes. Physicians typically reviewed a range of treatment options with patients. One unexpected outcome was the degree of involvement by patients, challenging or dismissing specific treatments. The meetings were more give-and-take than anticipated, suggesting situational, emotion-based circumstances entered into the decision as well. Unsurprisingly, the research client decided to step up awareness campaigns to ensure their product was always a proposed option and top-of-mind when the discussions occurred.

In terms of process, the lessons learned about mobile interviewing were also instructive. This approach enables communication while respondents are in the decision-making moment and an ability to gather quite a lot of qualitative (and quantitative) data at relatively low cost. The researchers did learn that intensive briefing was important before the study started as physicians are both busy and unfamiliar with this research technique. Similarly, incentives were useful and most effective if intermittent, not in one large package. The one aspect of depth interviews researchers reported missing was the ability to ask questions or probe more deeply. The voice memos were what they were; no additional information could be gained without going back to respondents later.

Lextant

Lextant is another qualitative research-oriented firm using innovative techniques. In one study, 27 "millennials" aged 20–30 were studied with the aim of better understanding that cohort. Respondents were asked to keep online records of meaningful experiences related to all facets of their lives. After several weeks, subjects participated in individual interviews. Researchers used a proprietary projective technique including standardized language and images, recording what respondents said about aspirations and desired experiences. The technique had the advantage of giving respondents time to reflect on their lives and what was important to them. Their answers were also open-ended but since prompted by a more structured tool, they could also be analyzed for similarities and patterns.

In another study, Lextant looked to discover "desired consumer experiences" for a pharmaceutical firm, specifically for vitamin supplements. Once again, the technique focused in on consumer aspirations and experiences. This time these aspects of the consumer psyche were examined in terms of product and package design. The sample was 48 consumers split equally across two countries. Preliminary activities were conducted online, capturing the aspirations of respondents (how they want to feel) and the benefits of feeling that way. In part, these feelings were captured by having consumers identify other brands providing such feelings (e.g. protected) and descriptors of those brands. Eventually, the online exercises identified certain product features and the attributes delivering those features and desired feelings. For example, a respondent feels their best every day because of a sense of protection delivered by a natural product with a textured surface.

The study then moved to a face-to-face stage, essentially group interviews but with hands-on activities built into the process. Respondents were asked to create an ideal self, based on visual prompts (e.g. photo of an athlete) and written descriptors. They were then asked to build an ideal product using images and physical objects including a variety of forms, sizes, textures, containers and so on. With all the data in hand, the analysts were able to isolate patterns. The patterns showed not only what respondents preferred in the product and its packaging but gave some insight into why, based on how their preferences were formed. The point was not to take features or attributes as given specifications (this is exploratory research, after all) but to be strategic and "inspirational". So not only were results obtained but, once again, some of the reasoning or emotions behind the results.

DISCUSSION #1

Both of these examples highlight some of the prominent trends apparent in exploratory, qualitative research. Several of these trends have a foot in big data and analytics, at least in some of the technologies associated with collecting and analyzing huge amounts of data.

Initially, notice the more traditional elements included in the SKIM and Lextant approaches. There are aspects of depth interviews in all of the examples, with physicians, millennials and pharmaceutical consumers answering open-ended questions. Some tendencies of a focus group are also apparent in the Lextant pharmaceutical study. Though individuals conducted their ideal product and packaging work on their own, they were all brought together in a single space, working side-by-side on the same project. Even without verbal communication (and one would imagine there was some), a group dynamic could develop, and this approach certainly mirrors the economic advantages of focus groups (all discussion and activity in the same place, making more efficient use of the researchers' and analysts' time). Though this was clearly not a traditional focus group, well-planned group interviews can create some of the same benefits.

Projective techniques are also prominent in the Lextant research. One of the main reasons to use a projective technique is to help respondents to express feelings they might not realize they have or may have trouble putting into words. If you ask someone straight out what their aspirations might be, you'll probably get some odd responses. Doing so by asking them about brands they admire or to pick pictures depicting their ideal self can be of immense help in leading them to a truer answer. And it does so in a manner that allows some comparison between respondents, providing a basis for pattern recognition even if statistical reliability remains beyond the capabilities of exploratory research.

Several things in the approaches are illustrative of new capabilities or current trends. Initially, the combination of techniques, sometimes in an innovative manner, is something we are seeing more frequently in current studies. Combining individual interviews with a group setting, combining online data collection with person-to-person administration, and combining observation with communication are all things that wouldn't necessarily be done if researchers were just picking a traditional approach and implementing it according to directions. So, in the case of the pharmaceutical group interview, researchers could not only watch the choices individuals made in creating, say, an innovative packaging concept. They could ask them about it. Not only what was done but also the why and wherefore of it, uncovering the underlying feelings.

All the studies show some aspect of gathering data over a longer time period. In the Lextant studies, with the preliminary work to understand the respondents (and help them understand themselves) and the later in-person interviews, the data-gathering process was stretched out. The case is similar with the physicians reporting numerous episodes over an even longer period of time. Often, studies will be done quickly so as to minimize any bias as the respondents figure out the purpose or the sponsor of the study. Bias can also come from external events that occur during the time of the data gathering (events in respondents' lives, events in the world). But more data gathering is being done over an extended time period, including multiple studies in some cases, so as to get a better insight into the flow of subjects' lives and options rather than snapshots. Bias can be managed in other ways such as hiding the true purpose with projective techniques and/or larger samples that wash out the impact of biasing events unique to individual respondents.

One issue with some traditional interviews and most focus groups is the artificiality of the setting. Face-to-face focus groups are typically conducted in specialized facilities with audio/video recording capabilities and a one-way mirror allowing observation by clients or researchers. Sometimes, respondents can take longer to get comfortable in such settings and open up. The ability to do the research in a setting that is more convenient and more like everyday life, such as the mobile interviews with physicians, can lead to more revealing responses. Similarly, as already pointed out, gaining responses in the moment can be more accurate than asking about state of mind some time later. The active nature of the setting in the pharmaceutical product and package design process would also put respondents at ease. With active engagement, subjects are likely to focus less on the artificiality of the setting and more on the task. Much like active learning in the classroom, hands-on tasks bring a different perspective and, often, a truer reaction.

Finally, the means of collecting and analyzing the data opens up new possibilities. Mobile use in interviews (and, in fact, mobile for all kinds of data gathering including surveys) is increasing, for many of the reasons we've already discussed. But it also allows researchers to take in unstructured data, such as text from interviews or video from group activities, and directly move it into databases and store it. For text, analytical tools, such as content analysis (cataloguing text according to key words and concepts) can also be used to review and study it and on a much greater scale than was previously possible.

Similarly, the Lextant studies could use both observation and communication, and it's very likely the observation was preserved with video. Once again, this type of unstructured data can be moved quickly into information systems, stored, and later searched and analyzed with contemporary analytical tools. Video can take up considerable amounts of storage space, making analysis difficult. But, again, this is one of the big steps forward in applying marketing analytics to this type of big data. The analytical tools are made to allow study of exactly these types of huge databases.

Because of the growing ease, efficiency, and cost savings in analyzing unstructured big data, the idea of extending sample sizes to much larger levels (500 physicians) and/or collecting detailed observations of long face-to-face or virtual sessions (product and package design for vitamins) now makes sense. While a larger sample size wouldn't necessarily push a study into statistically significant descriptive research design territory, it could. But even if remaining a qualitative exploratory design, the larger samples can obtain a taste of a wider range of inputs and potential insights. Diversity of ideas and insights can lead to better conclusions and decisions. When looking for something new, interesting and unexpected, sampling from more sources is typically better than sampling from fewer. So the ability to use technological tools to gather more data and store it is just as important for qualitative research as it is for more quantitative approaches. Moreover, even if not statistically significant from quantitative hypothesis testing, the larger sample sizes can still lend a sense of grounding to the results – that the insights might be common to groups of subjects, perhaps large groups of subjects, not just single individuals.

Everything isn't always positive, of course, when settling on the details of a research design. Tradeoffs tend to be present, and changing a technique to improve one aspect of the study may harm others. The beauty of some of the newer choices can be multiple advantages to only a new disadvantage or two, essentially looking for the best of both worlds by combining tools to emphasize the positives. But downsides should be recognized.

In these cases, we've already noted that "in-the-moment" interviewing and independent reporting make follow-up or probing questions difficult. With no interviewer there, the physicians in the SKIM study simply say what they want to say and then log off. Any probing would be in follow-up questions days, weeks or even months after the original memo, severely curtailing effectiveness. In all of these studies the researchers are not hidden, neither is the purpose of the study. Further, whenever studies take place over a longer period of time, there is a concern about respondents becoming "fans" of the brand (if it is not hidden). Here, there is no indication the study sponsor was revealed but the possibility of subjects figuring it out and reacting is present. And these are all essentially interviews without the true dynamics of a focus group (only subtler aspects of a group in the vitamin study, as mentioned). Researchers may not have intended the dynamic, which is fine, and it certainly wasn't present at all with the physicians and only at a lower level with the Lextant studies.

WHAT'S NEW #2?

Culture Concepts

Culture Concepts and an independent strategy consultant constructed an innovative approach to studying the market for nutrition bars for 1-For-1 Foods (1F1). The small start-up company's business model was to copy the Buy-One-Give-One (BOGO) social responsibility angle of TOMS Shoes (and others), donating a nutrition bar to a homeless shelter for every bar purchased by a consumer. Reasoning that their target consumers not only cared about health and fitness but also social responsibility, 1F1 commissioned several (pro bono) marketing research studies.

Initially, the researchers monitored social media chatter for an understanding of what their likely segment had to say about these topics, looking to identify themes in the social interaction. From that base, they constructed two ethnographic studies. In the first, the researchers identified TOMS users, six 20–30-year-olds, already acquainted, and shadowed them on a shopping trip and to dinner. The observers listened in on conversations and observed matters like dress (who wore TOMS, who didn't) and behavior. This included insights like preferring the TOMS a little scuffed up, signaling that the shoes were worn on a regular basis. Researchers were also able to identify a number of salient characteristics of the group, including how they felt about political/societal issues and other brands of interest.

The second ethnographic study was in a more innovative setting as researchers accompanied a group on a hiking trip. Ten friends, identified as health bar consumers, were recruited. The group was male and female and represented a wider range of ages. The plan was developed in consultation with the group, so they apparently knew the study had to do with health bars. Researchers were able to observe respondent behavior over three days, capturing some video, including social interactions and use of the product. Further, they were able to listen in on conversations and exchanges. Most importantly, the researchers were able to gain insight into the place and relative importance of health bars in the hikers' lives. One important finding was the social aspect of consumption, eating the bars while in a group, and statements about what health bar consumption portrayed to others.

Doyle Research & Associates

Doyle Research & Associates used several approaches to develop a better understanding of the car buying process. Research objectives included observing onsite experiences at the dealer that impacted the potential buyer, identifying key moments in the purchase decision, and determining what consumers really want from the process. If you've studied complex decision-making related to consumer behavior, you know car buying is an expensive, non-routine purchase, so buyers tend to take their time, accumulating and processing more information than they do with routine or impulse purchases.

In this case, Doyle used a mix of new and old techniques, trying to collect data from various perspectives that could then be analyzed for insights. Initially, screen-sharing webcam interviews (6 respondents) were done with prospective buyers so researchers could see what their internet search practices looked like matched with conversations about their search reasoning. Interviews were also done at dealerships. Rather than traditional intercept discussions, researchers used a locator technology (Doyle has its own proprietary version) to identify phones in the immediate vicinity and request an interview. In this way, they were likely to get more cooperation (the innovative approach intrigues respondents) and catch them in-the-moment, much like the oncology study discussed earlier. The dealership experience would be fresh in respondents' minds as they were asked questions about what was happening. Interview responses were by text and subjects were also asked for a selfie and some pictures of the dealership. Follow-up chats took place on a discussion board dedicated to the research.

Ethnographic research was also used. In one part of the study, 18 ninety-minute in-home interviews were conducted with recent or soon-to-be buyers. Questions "delve[d] into all the nuances, emotions and complexities of the process and purchases" (Morgan, 2015). Video was employed to store the data for later use, including salesperson training. Six in-home respondents then participated in ride-alongs to the dealerships to document and answer more questions about their impressions of the onsite buying experience.

The main conclusions of the study showed the increasing use of more contemporary communication techniques (something car dealerships aren't always very good at) and a desire for more transparency in the process. Consumers are used to being able to research and buy online with a few keystrokes, so the opacity of car buying and the need to deal with a less-than-forthcoming salesperson rubs a lot of consumers the wrong way. Everyone knows consumers don't much like the car buying process. But this research provided new insights as to why as well as some suggestions about what to do about it.

Deprivation Studies

Deprivation studies are a specific type of projective technique. Again, they aren't necessarily new though some new applications are possible in our current data gathering and processing environment. The basic idea is to take away something to which the subjects are accustomed (deprive them) and that they value. By their reactions, you can determine the value of the item. In marketing research, the item would tend to be a specific experience, product, or brand.

As noted, deprivation studies are not a new creation. One of the best-known studies took place a decade ago, when Crispin Porter + Bogusky, working with Burger King, took the Whopper off the menu in selected stores. Burger King had been doing forms of deprivation studies for years, asking some of its most loyal customers to forgo the Whopper for a period of time, reporting in a food diary what they ate (and, in particular, what they ate instead of the Whopper). Researchers knew their core customers already went to Burger King five times a month, on average, and a little over twice that to other fast-food restaurants.

The "Whopper Freakout" campaign applied this research to an advertising campaign, both television and online (still readily available with a quick search). This particular set-up was not actual research but illustrates the value of the technique. Stores in Las Vegas were staffed with actors, had the Whopper crossed off the menu, and caught customer reactions on video. Predictably, some were dramatic, making the final cut of the ad. Researchers ran a second version of the scenario in which they served customers ordering the Whopper a competing product instead. Everyone the researchers could catch was debriefed, and those used in the ad signed release forms. A few irate customers left before researchers could catch them, illustrating one of the downsides of this type of research.

More recent examples of the technique include ESPN, whose depriva-tion study presented at the 2011 Market Research Annual Conference was blogged about at www.relevantinsights.com. Sixty ESPN users were recruited (and paid) to go without the channel for a month during the football season. Thirty used only the cable channel and 30 used the channel and other ESPN media choices. Respondents reported back through video and audio diaries, focus groups, depth interviews, and pre-/ post-questionnaires. The research sought to capture "vivid illustrations of how consumers felt about the brand" and what they watched when ESPN wasn't available. From such results, ESPN felt it could make better deci-sions about its strategy for delivering content on multiple platforms.

DISCUSSION #2

Once again, we can summarize the characteristics of these examples into a more organized picture about current practice concerning exploratory research design. Some of the points are similar to those made earlier, though more fully explained. Others show us something different.

Initially, the anecdotes again show a mix and match of traditional and more cutting-edge methodologies. Ethnographic studies are present in two of them, including depth interviews and observation. Standard depth interviews are also apparent, especially in the car buying research. Projective techniques, of course, were presented as a topic of interest in and of themselves.

But these more traditional approaches are again more complex than the vanilla manner in which we think of them. Using current communication technology, it's possible to conduct the interviews and ethnographic visits via the web or by means of mobile devices. Indeed, potential contacts can be identified and recruited via mobile, both catching them at the time they are making decisions and approaching them in a more interesting manner that intrigues them. Response rates can go up because of the novelty. The approaches also show different ways of taking in the data, not just capturing a transcript of the conversation but also photos, video and other more unstructured data. Indeed, video diaries are common with ethnographic and/or deprivation studies, capturing in-the-moment feelings and easily accomplished with mobile devices. The entire experience can be described with different media and points-of-view.

As this can be done fairly easily and in a cost-effective manner today, the second point to be made is that larger sample sizes are again possible. Both of the ethnographic studies mentioned here involved small samples (one was pro bono, so was probably planned to be small and inexpensive) but it's easy to see how they could be scaled up without too much difficulty. Especially interesting would be efforts in the car buying study to follow consumers as they browse and shop online and/or increase the geo-located recruiting and interviewing methods at the dealerships. Technology would allow those aspects of the study to be repeated and captured quite easily, then stored for later analysis. Similarly with the nutrition bar study, once the events (shop-along or camping trip) are arranged, capturing days of interaction with the respondents is easily done and processed.

The case is best made with the projective techniques, however, especially the Burger King example. In the ESPN case, the sample size is what one often sees in exploratory work, with 30 respondents in each category, though that could also be ramped up to higher numbers fairly easily (the interesting nature of the research and generous compensation would help). But doing something provocative in the consumer's environment and then capturing reactions over time, as with Whopper Freakout, is a way to capture dozens or even hundreds of responses in relatively short order. Once again, both observation and communication can be employed, and the audio and video produced by such interactions is easily processed, stored and analyzed with contemporary information technology tools.

All of the examples show innovative use of prompts for gaining a reaction from respondents. Further, these prompts tend to be oriented to the real world, taking the data gathering out of artificial environments. Contrasting with a traditional focus group or depth interview at an artificial facility, each of these cases goes to the subjects in their world in order to gain feedback. Moreover, once they have identified potential respondents, they utilize unique and interesting prompts to get them to participate and/or react.

Accompanying brand-loyal TOMS consumers on a shopping trip or health-centered adults on a camping trip is a way to stimulate their curiosity, gain cooperation, and place them in environments in which they are comfortable. Making an initial contact with a car buyer via text as they're in the dealership is also unexpected and intriguing as would be shop-alongs and photo documentation at the dealership. Challenging hard-core ESPN users to go without it for a period of time, especially during the NFL season during which so many are passionate about highlights, would spark their curiosity. And, of course, eliminating the most popular and well-known menu item at Burger King is bound to get an interesting reaction. Far from the difficulties marketing research sometimes faces in terms of gaining respondents for myriad stale interviews and questionnaires, these types of innovative techniques can get potential recruits interested or even excited about participating. And if they are participating in the field, in their own real world, the results can be particularly insightful.

Indeed, the format of some of these studies actually looks very similar to what you'll see when we take a closer look at experimental research design. Experiments are usually carefully controlled (especially if in the laboratory or an artificial environment). Even in the field, researchers try to keep as many variables constant as possible so that when a single experimental variable is changed, they can track the impact. In experimental research design, this is quantitative, measuring the results from a sample large enough to establish both impact and causation. Here, the metrics are qualitative, but the structure is similar. Go into the real world. Change a single variable (and, in the field, you hope no other variables change and bias the result). Note the impact. So, set up a Burger King, change the menu item, and see what happens. As we've talked about in other cases where techniques are cross-fertilizing one another, some of the lines between research designs are also blurring as innovative analysts find interesting ways to accumulate insights.

WHAT'S NEW #3?

Gamification is a concept that is self-explanatory but at the same time more complex than it seems. Research projects have always been a balance between identifying and relentlessly pursuing specific information vs. finding ways to keep respondents engaged. Gamification is simply a tool to make information gathering more interesting for the subjects. But behind such tools is some deeper thinking about honest responses and how the context of research can be used to make a difference.

As we've mentioned a few times already, some research-gathering environments can be antiseptic and imposing. Asking questions in focus group facilities, interview rooms in malls, or similar spots doesn't necessarily put respondents at ease. Neither do carefully constructed questions with impeccable wording (there are reasons we do that, but these can sound awkward to the subjects). As Warnock and Gantz put it, participating in marketing research shouldn't be like taking an exam, it should be fun and entertaining. So if you can make the process and instrument more engaging, put the respondents more at ease, you will likely find them more willing to talk.

A good amount of the guidance on gamification flows from surveys and more descriptive or causal research that we'll be covering in upcoming chapters. But gamification applies to qualitative, exploratory research as well. And it may be even more powerful in circumstances asking for open-ended responses. When individuals are comfortable, they tend to open up more, go more deeply into stories or memories, and generally reveal more about themselves. Gamification, in its various forms, can make individuals more comfortable.

Gamification tactics include gaming elements but also other approaches. Tom Ewing from Brainjuicer suggests that the main point is to make the process fun for subjects while having the additional advantage of enhancing the creativity of researchers, making them think more deeply about their own approach to harvesting information. The trend toward more gamification comes partly from Kahneman's rational/ emotional decision-making dichotomy mentioned earlier. In order to get to the emotional feelings behind decisions, gamification tools tend to take individuals more into the area of feeling rather than reasoning. Choosing a smiley face logo as a response is different from reading through text answers a, b, c or d. Further, as social media have become a bigger part of consumers' lives, individuals have become accustomed to competing, collaborating and engaging with friends and acquaintances. Ewing uses the example of the app Foursquare as an illustration, where users compete to have the most check-ins at locations, with the top-ranked earning titles like Mayor. So this type of competitive/ collaborative behavior is familiar to quite a number of potential research participants.

The characteristics of gamification are varied, and are not all necessarily associated with gaming; the applications are broader than the topic would apply. These can include, according to Warnock and Gantz:

- images (instrument aesthetics, response formats such as sliders or drag and drop, images on card sorts, brand logos);
- competitive elements (time limits, comparisons, early response bonuses);
- projective techniques, as already discussed;
- feedback, often immediate (this is how you compare to others, this is the category in which your responses would place you);
- rules (timing, number of required responses for open-ended, etc.);
- personalization (relate to individual experiences)

Just about all of these elements could be part of any research design, but Susan Fader of Fader & Associates has additional recommendations specifically for qualitative, exploratory studies. Part of that process is in recruiting participants. Instead of a list of screening questions to get specific types of respondents, she recommends a more inviting process, posing the research as a participative game by explaining the rules, obtaining buy-in immediately to the nature and content of the exercise, explicitly identifying rewards up-front, and personalizing the questions. Making the environment more comfortable can also help by employing techniques such as open seating (rather than assigned seats, including for a discussion moderator), activities to keep respondents busy while waiting, and providing rewards with games of chance for early arrivals. Using the example of a study on sexually transmitted diseases (STD), she notes the difficulty of recruiting a diverse sample (across demographics, sexual orientations, sexual behaviors, condom usage, number of sexual partners, and types of STDs) and getting open, honest responses on a very private topic. Rather than asking blunt questions to qualify respondents, researchers simply asked how they lost their virginity. Although nervous about asking, interviewers reported back that respondents were very talkative, going into rich detail and leading to discussions that organically answered most of the screening questions. Personalizing the study subject in this manner led to honest and detailed results. This comfort level also fed into the focus groups themselves, again leading to very open and enlightening conversations.

As should now be clear, gamification can include a number of aspects. Some are exactly what you'd expect from a term like gamification, they add elements of competition and gaming to the process. But quite a number of others go beyond those elements, making participation in research fun and interesting like a game even without the typical aspects of one. If successful, subjects are more engaged with the process, improving response rates and the quality and richness of the feedback. If successful in involving the respondent, such techniques can put them back into their decision-making context, letting more of the subconscious into responses (as when emotional thought influences rational thought in real life). Anything that makes the participants feel more comfortable with the situation and less like a lab rat can lead to better results.

PRESCRIPTION FOR EXPLORATORY MARKETING ANALYTICS

The nature of exploratory research design puts some limits on what big data can contribute, at least in terms of respondent totals. In later chapters we'll discuss studies involving huge numbers of observations and, although bigger than traditional levels in many cases, contemporary exploratory research still doesn't look for statistically reliable results or the required number of respondents needed to generate those results. But that doesn't mean that big data, analytics, and the trends fueling their growth don't have a lot to do with new directions in exploratory research design.

Although the number of respondents might still be kept relatively low, the amount of information that can be taken in by modern technology has still increased sharply. As noted in a number of the examples in this chapter, researchers can capture and store data from multiple perspectives, with multiple methods of administration, and with full detail. The multiple perspectives include both observation and communication in many cases. It's not hard to capture an in-depth observation exercise with audio and video, pairing it with any additional questions that might be asked during or after the research. Further, multiple types of observation can be employed (e.g. physical observation paired with observation of web activities) as can multiple types of communication (e.g. video diaries with real-time interviews). And, finally, researchers can capture the full context of episodes, so that a record is available not just of eating a nutrition bar but the activities and conversations that take place around the consumption event and several days surrounding it. And, yes, bigger samples can be completed at reasonable cost, useful in many cases even in exploratory research. All of these things take considerably more data storage but, again, that's really not a problem in today's world. Researchers should consider the full range of tools available to them in accomplishing a research objective, being open to using multiple approaches and taking in full context data.

Current technology has also opened up the ability to do more unobtrusive and/or natural-setting qualitative research. This goes naturally with more observation research, particularly in online environments, but it can be valuable for qualitative research as well as quantitative. Social media chatter, activity on apps or in web browsing, use of loyalty programs or other tracked activity, and location tracking can all be done without the subject being explicitly aware (most of us know that such monitoring is at least possible). Or when data are collected with the knowledge of the subject, when it is done in the course of regular, everyday activities, it's much less likely that reflecting on the circumstances will happen and bias the results. Gamification, as just discussed, illustrates one approach. When subjects' minds are on an interesting task, in a comfortable environment they tend to be much more open and responsive. When subjects feel as if they are taking a boring exam, the results will be just what you would expect. Pay attention to the ethical considerations, we'll talk about those later, but take advantage of opportunities to decrease respondent self-awareness. That includes dropping their awareness to zero, so they are totally in the dark that research on them is taking place, when possible and ethical.

One important way to be unobtrusive and natural is to use existing data that may already be in the system. While a lot of the interest in big data is about collecting quantitative data, including transactional, communication, and web-/mobile-based results, there can also be considerable qualitative data available as well. In particular, observations of customer activities, particularly virtual activities, are routinely collected and can be monitored on an individual basis, providing the depth concerning those activities that we look for in exploratory work. Social media can and should be constantly monitored and stored. Again, the full nature of the comments can be explored for exploratory insights. Other customer communications with the firm, in whatever form, are also usually captured and stored. And, as noted earlier, third party commercial data are also available, especially those describing consumer attitudes or behavior in specific contexts (Nielsen and media consumption) or specific industries (IMS Health and health care).

Review of qualitative data is also impacted by big data and analytics. Although many of the processing tools used for big databases don't really apply, some of the analysis concepts do. Initially, recall that what we've been calling unstructured data (text, audio, images, video) can be digitized and stored in databases. Consequently, it can be analyzed using some of the tabulation and cross-tabulation techniques discussed earlier, cutting the data by variables of interest to see what differences or associations might be apparent. Even without a large number of respondents, the unstructured data still holds a lot of detail. Analytical software could cut video captures of shopping behavior, for example, by time of day, location, whether the shopper is alone or accompanied and so on. While there may only be 50 video snippets, the accompanying database could turn out to be quite large. So the video pieces could be watched by analysts, recording their conclusions. Or the pieces could be processed, looking for those similarities and differences among the context information. Or, most likely, analysts would examine such qualitative data in both ways.

We also have some specific analytical processes for unstructured data. Content analysis has long been applied to text, with humans identifying and classifying key words, looking for rates of occurrence to highlight important concepts repeatedly mentioned. Analytical software can do such tasks today and, in fact, that's exactly what word clouds are about. Word clouds are just another way to present content analysis findings. Other techniques are also available to convert qualitative data to quantitative data, allowing a fuller set of analysis tools to be employed. Social media studies, for example, often categorize postings by sentiment (good, bad, neutral) or other aspects. Once done, data monitoring can track metrics such as the positive sentiment trend of a brand across all social media. If the brand image takes a dip, the actual postings are stored away and available for analysis by researchers who want to take a closer look. One thing to keep in mind, however, is that the adaptation of qualitative to quantitative isn't always totally accurate. As the saying goes, the internet doesn't get irony or sarcasm. So a snarky reply might get classified improperly as a positive when, in fact, any human reading it would understand the negativity. Context and human interpretation can still be important. Even so, although we don't associate qualitative, unstructured data with spreadsheets and analytics, our ability to take in and examine exploratory results in ever more scope and scale is there. It again often comes down to familiarity with available tools and the willingness to try new approaches in new situations.

Even in the qualitative sector represented by exploratory research design, big data and marketing analytics are having a substantial impact on research. Decision-makers should think about the full and growing array of techniques, media and analysis available to them. In many ways, it's in the exploratory domain that the most innovative and interested advances are happening. We can analyze ever more results in ever more detail, capturing unexpected insights from all kinds of sources.

BIBLIOGRAPHY

Beatty, S. and C. Hymowitz (2000), "How MTV stays tuned into teens", *The Wall Street Journal*, 21 March, available at http://www.wsj.com/articles/SB953594786214293099, accessed 30 October 2016.

Bennett, D. (2015), "What would Heidegger do?", *Bloomberg Businessweek*, 21 February, pp. 52–6.

Dignan, L. (2016), "Cognizant buys stake in ReD Associates, aims to meld digital with social sciences", *ZDNet*, 28 April, available at http://www.zdnet.com/article/cognizant-buys-stake-in-red-associates-aims-to-meld-digital-with-social-science/, accessed 15 September 2016.

Economist (2013), "The Adidas method", 24 August, online edition.

Ewing, T. (2012), "Where gamification came from and why it is here to stay", *Quirk's Marketing Research Review*, March, available at http://www.quirks.com/articles/where-gamification-came-from-and-why-it-could-be-here-to-stay, accessed 30 October 2016.

Fader, S. (2012), "Getting in the game: New ways of gamifying qualitative research", *Quirk's Marketing Research Review*, December, available at http://www.quirks.com/articles/new-ways-of-gamifying-qualitative-research, accessed 30 October 2016.

Flessner, L. and M. Gage (2013), "Insight-driven innovation for health care products", powerpoint deck, available at www.lextant.com, accessed 15 February 2014.

Jasperson, J. and R. Tonar (2013), "Creative ethnography helps small nutrition-bar start-up find its path", *Quirk's Marketing Research Review*, February, p. 28.

Lux-Hawkins, S.L. (2015), "Qualitative approach aims to have Millennials dig deep", *Quirk's Marketing Research Review*, February, p. 54.

Madsbjerg, C. and M.B. Rasmussen (2014), "An anthropologist walks into a bar", *Harvard Business Review*, **92**(3), 80–88.

Mora, M. (2011), "How can market research regain its mojo? Watch ESPN", 21 June, available at www.relevantinsights.com, accessed 15 September 2014.

Morgan, A. (2015), "Baby, you can drive my car", *Alert! (Market Research Association)*, 12 November, online edition.

Roos, E. (2015), "Conducting in-the-moment mobile research with physicians", *Quirk's Marketing Research Review*, February, p. 42.

Vranica, S. (2008), "Hey, no Whopper on the menu?!", *The Wall Street Journal*, 8 February, online edition.

Warnock, S. and J.S. Gantz (2016), "Does gamification provide relief from survey-taking torture?", *Quirk's Marketing Research Review*, 5 October, available at http://www.quirks.com/articles/does-gamification-offer-relief-from-survey-taking-torture, accessed 30 October 2016.

3

Descriptive research design

Descriptive research design has much more obvious signs of the impact of big data and marketing analytics than what we saw in the last chapter. The links to what is happening with exploratory research designs, however, are also clear. In fact, the lines between qualitative and quantitative research are blurring somewhat as the ability grows to collect large amounts of qualitative data and process it more objectively. As we'll see, sometimes similar approaches are used, the differences being more in the intention of the research: to uncover new insights (exploratory) or to support a developing hypothesis (descriptive).

ASSESSING ADVERTISING

One illuminating example of these and other trends in practice is found in advancements in advertising evaluation. In choosing what advertising to run, marketers try to predict effectiveness. Whatever the communication objectives (awareness, knowledge, emotional arousal), firms spending money on advertising want some idea of whether or not those objectives were achieved. Consequently, the ads are assessed before completion and launch.

This can be done on a qualitative basis. Individual or small groups can be shown ads and discuss their impressions of the message and impact of the communication. But given the risk levels of big-budget advertising, firms often want more statistical reliability in the evaluation and so go for larger samples and more quantitative metrics. Kantar Millward Brown is a marketing research provider that has made a name for itself as a destination for advertising assessment and consulting. It evaluates advertising with viewings and questions designed to tease out the level of engagement with the ad. A few years ago, it produced a proprietary system (ABCD) to assess the viral potential of an ad based on a 50-item survey asking respondents about awareness, buzz, celebrity and distinctiveness.

Evolving approaches exist, however, whose originators believe will provide better, or at least more complete results. One of the best-known television ads in history, for example, the Cadbury Gorilla commercial (easily searched if you want to take a look), reportedly scored relatively poorly on Millward Brown's metrics. In particular, awareness and brand appeal were weak for women and only average for men. Some observers believe this has to do with focusing on the rational appeal of the ad rather than the emotional. Daniel Kahneman's System 1/System 2, emotional/rational concept was mentioned earlier in this book and comes into play here again. Newer approaches seek to tease out more of the emotional pull of advertising.

BrainJuicer, for example, employs a scale of eight faces portraying different emotions. The Cadbury Gorilla ad scored very highly for the emotional portrayals signifying surprise and happiness. Similarly, Decode's approach is to associate concepts with images and include a time metric, with quicker associations signaling stronger associations. When Decode evaluated the Cadbury Gorilla, it found relatively high scores for enjoyment and security, lower for adventure and excitement.

Even more recent work brings observation studies into play. Facial tracking techniques can be used to monitor changes in a subject's face as they view advertising, with very subtle changes being both measurable and significant. Emotient, for example, developed an algorithm from hundreds of thousands of participants on video. Capable of capturing and processing 90 000 pieces of data per video still, the software recognizes particular emotions from happiness to anger. Similarly, Affectiva has collected 2.4 million facial videos, also able to identify feelings from subtle changes in expression. In an app from *The Wall Street Journal* demonstrating Affectiva's technology (http://graphics.wsj.com/data-mining-of-emotions//), you can see a simple version of the technology as it tracks an individual viewing a video over a 30-second span. Quantitative data on surprise, confusion and other perceived emotions are tracked over time. The techniques not only quantify the overall reaction to an advertisement, but also what specific moments in the video spur what specific emotions.

This sort of advance changes a lot of things concerning how we view assessing advertising effectiveness. It captures responses that subjects may not even realize they are experiencing. Rather than asking about feelings, observation reveals respondents' true feelings about an ad. It captures such data quantitatively, making it easy to store, process and analyze. And it is able to do so in a different manner. Traditionally, advertising was tested by bringing subjects into a facility, screening video with the ads or with both content and embedded ads, and then assessing reaction to the ads. Sometimes this was straightforward and the respondents knew the research concerned how they felt about the ad. Sometimes, the true purpose was hidden (by including content) so that the ad did not appear to be the main focus. But it invariably involved assembling respondents in an artificial environment and asking questions.

With the new technology, the ads can be delivered online to virtually anywhere. The home, on a mobile to respondents on the move, or really anywhere they might be living their normal lives. The reactions are captured unobtrusively when they switch on their device's camera, and the reactions are mainly involuntary, so the purpose of the research doesn't necessarily need to be hidden.

In addition, researchers can collect responses quickly from all over the country or all over the world. All it takes is the 30 or 60 seconds necessary to screen the ad, and that can be done simultaneously with as many viewers as can be recruited. Adding questions to the process for even further insights wouldn't really slow things down appreciably or add substantial costs. Contrast that approach with the need to have an interviewer present to collect responses onsite from individuals or a group. The ability to obtain a large number of responses quickly and efficiently has been amplified considerably.

And that is part of the impact of big data and marketing analytics on research. The data collection is usually easier. The insights can be deeper and more reliable. The sample sizes can be very large. And the data covering a wider range of variables can be stored, processed and analyzed in new ways as well.

DESCRIPTIVE RESEARCH DESIGN

Descriptive research design is typically characterized as large sample, quantitative research designed to "shed light" on a hypothesis (short of being able to confirm it). In relation to exploratory research, an insight gained from a more in-depth, open-ended approach could be given support by a descriptive finding. An organization can learn whether an idea is just held by a few individuals that isn't pertinent or whether it is something widespread that should be acted upon. Descriptive research establishes credibility. Again, however, descriptive cannot "prove" anything is true or untrue; you need an experiment for that level of certainty.

Table 3.1   Useful terminology

Questionnaire/ Survey	Primary means of communication research for descriptive studies. Instrument with questions administered to respondents.	
Method of Administration	Refers to means of delivering instrument to respondent (means of administering questionnaire)	
	Mail	Instrument sent and returned by mail. Rarely used any more.
	Telephone	Generally refers to landline, instrument is administered by phone. Very popular twenty years ago, declining in popularity as individuals answering and participating are unlikely to be representative.
	Person-to-person	Door-to-door (rare), interviews (some business applications), and mall intercepts (still used, including other locations like airports). Administered by a questioner, in person. Allows for longer instruments, product demonstrations, and other hands-on interactions.
	Internet	Very popular and growing. Does not require a real person asking questions and has most advantages of any of the other techniques including low cost, speed and geographical flexibility. Only real downsides are ensuring identity of participant and inability to demonstrate.
	Mobile	Popular and growing even more quickly. All the advantages of internet administration plus ability to do "in-the-moment" surveys.
Response Patterns (covered in more detail in a later chapter)	Manner in which respondents answer questions	
	Open-ended	Respondent can answer anything, unlimited space
	Multiple choice	Typically referred to as dichotomous (only two choices) or multichotomous (more than two choices), allows a limited range of responses. Easy to process.
	Self-report scales	Frequently used scales (essentially multichotomous), often for specific purposes. Have advantages of being validated from many previous uses and respondents are likely to be familiar with them. Prominent examples are Likert (intensity of feeling scale) and Semantic Differential (perception of brand attributes).
	Numerical	As it implies, response is quantitative

Like the other research designs, descriptive research design can have existing secondary data or new observation or communication data. Positive characteristics of the research design include closed-ended responses (enabling large samples and workable tabulation of results), more objectivity (again, response patterns and less influence of interviewers and subjective analysts), potentially quick results, and low cost per respondent. Less positive characteristics include the loss of depth (no probing, no unexpected responses, no flexibility or open-endedness in questioning), the need for a large sample (for statistical reliability), and a high total cost. These distinctions have blurred a bit. As noted, technology and new methods have enabled the collection of large amounts of open-ended results (convertible to quantitative data) quickly and at reasonable cost. But as a general guide, they illustrate the difference in purpose and approach between exploratory designs and descriptive designs.

Secondary or existing data is much more prevalent with descriptive research designs than is the case with exploratory. Since many firms are becoming interested in ongoing, dependable evidence on consumer characteristics, opinions or behavior, quite a number of commercial data providers have emerged. These providers can provide data on a regular basis or to answer a new question in a specific study, and several are quite well-known. Nielsen, for example, provides periodic data on media consumption. This includes not only the well-known television ratings but everything from books, to gaming, to Twitter. Nielsen also has several less well-known (at least to the general public) services including comprehensive retail transaction data, tracking details about what is sold by product, brand, price, etc. from participating stores. NPD Group provides similar transaction data but from throughout the supply chain, including manufacturers' shipments, wholesaler transactions, and the retail end. Nielsen also provides data from its Claritas Prizm service, a database combining zip code data with consumer behavior characteristics (Prizm can describe the demographics and psychographics of consumers in specific zip code locations).

Google Analytics is also a well-known and widely used commercial provider, collecting and selling data on website usage, browsing behavior and e-commerce. Several providers monitor and report on social media activity, including Radian6 and Trackur. Data are collected on brand mentions across reviews, blogs, Facebook, Twitter, and other platforms. Interestingly, the data are quantitative even though the underlying texts (available to review for deeper insights) are qualitative. Commercial researchers specializing by industry also exist, including IMS (healthcare) and Forrester (technology). As you should immediately realize, purchasing this existing data is usually much quicker and much cheaper than trying to gather it yourself. The data also tend to be longitudinal, collected over time, showing changes and allowing comparisons across different time periods. In addition, these types of providers often have relationships allowing them to gather data on all or almost all competitors in a market, something that would be near impossible for a solitary firm.

Observation studies are a growing part of descriptive research. At one time, observation research on the scale necessary for descriptive results could take a very long time as individual observers would need to watch behaviors until the sample grew to an appropriate size. For shopper patterns, for example, trackers would actually sketch out and time the path a shopper took through a grocery store. Newer data gathering tools have made observation much quicker and much easier.

For individual companies, this has often meant customer observation. Your cable or satellite provider, for example, has a tremendous amount of data on the characteristics and behavior of its subscribers. The case is similar for any service or media source you access on the web or on mobile. Facebook has reams of data about its individual users. But the change that probably best illustrates the booming trend in customer observation data is found in loyalty programs, as discussed in the first chapter. These can be web-based (Amazon) or omnichannel (Tesco, Caesar's) but when customers identify themselves with a card or in some other way, it allows the collection of follow-on data concerning everything they do after that point. This can be a tremendous amount of data, collected not just on consumer groups but on individually identifiable consumers. And, of course, it can be aggregated in order to provide descriptive results.

Descriptive communication techniques generally begin and end with questionnaires (surveys). By definition, descriptive research looks for closed-ended, quantifiable data. And the best way to do that is with a questionnaire with those types of response patterns. And since it is a communication technique, we ask those questions. Everyone is familiar with surveys, and traditional marketing research courses often comprehensively cover question selection, response patterns (dichotomous, multiple choice/multichotomous, frequently used scales, etc.), and question sequencing. Much of that theory hasn't changed much, though you'll see in some of the examples covered here that response choices can be more interesting and engage with the use of some newer technologies, including gamification, visualization, drag and drop and so on.

These respondent engagement aspects can be important as communication techniques are uniquely able to delve into unobservable matters such as motivation, attitude, awareness, brand preference, past events and other things that occur only in the head of respondents. There are, however, concerns specific to communication. For one, gaining cooperation can be difficult. Subjects must agree to complete a sometimes lengthy questionnaire about a subject in which they may or may not have an interest. Moreover, with an explosion in surveys (you've probably noticed that almost every event you attend or major purchase you make now has a survey about what you thought of it), there is a sense of "survey fatigue" setting in among potential respondents. Any communication effort with an interviewer also has the possibility of bias from how the questions are presented or even from non-verbal expressions or gestures.

These concerns are one reason why the method of administration can be an important choice for questionnaires. Method of administration refers to how we conduct the survey and how we reach the respondents: traditional choices include person-to-person, mail and telephone. In recent years web-based administration has been growing rapidly because of numerous advantages over the more traditional choices. Even more recently, interest in mobile administration has started as well. Choice about administration usually revolves around ease of identifying respondents, response rates, respondent convenience, geographical coverage, cost, speed, anonymity, survey complexity, and ability to demonstrate (e.g. try a product). Internet administration is burgeoning because it comes top for almost every one of those aspects, except perhaps demonstration. It is fast, efficient, can be done at the convenience of subjects who also seem more receptive to doing surveys online. Complex question patterns (if yes, go to Q#34, if no, go to Q #46) can be programmed in, and some technological tricks can be used to make the survey more engaging. Meanwhile, mail is almost gone as is telephone in our age of do-not-call lists, caller ID, and diminishing landlines. Person-to-person is still used in specific applications like mall intercepts and, especially, for product demonstrations but is obviously slower, more expensive, and in other ways less attractive for a lot of applications. Mobile is seeing a lot of growth because it has many of the same advantages as internet surveys and is also capable of "in-the-moment" communications as discussed in the previous chapter. Mobile penetration (percentage of population using the technology) is also three times that of computers worldwide, opening the way to reach different segments of the population beyond those available just through the web.

Descriptive research can be extremely important in developing quantitative evidence supporting qualitative insights concerning customer attitudes,

behavior, intentions, preferences, and all sorts of other key marketing questions. Effective techniques exist for observing subjects or communicating
with them (or both). If done with a well-constructed, sizable sample and
administered properly, these studies can provide statistically reliable results
upon which decision-makers can act with some confidence. They are a critical
tool for marketers, especially in an age of big data and marketing analytics.

WHAT'S NEW #1?

What's new in the area of descriptive research? Quantitative studies are
where big data changes have had their most visible impact, both in terms
of the amount of data gathered and how it has been applied. Some new
developments have already been covered earlier in the discussions, specifically the rise of observation tools, changes in preferred methods of
administration, and respondent engagement. In addition, as some of the
exploratory research techniques are applied to larger samples in a more
structured way, many of those can become descriptive research (e.g. social
media observation). But considerably more innovation exists in this area,
and we'll draw it all out in some illustrative examples.

Shopping Apps

Shopping apps have mushroomed as smartphones have become ubiquitous. Many consumers use them for information on products, download-
ing promotional offers, and updating loyalty program information. Some
of the most popular allow consumers to create shopping lists and store
accompanying digital coupons.

In some ways, these apps are a move to combat "showrooming", when
consumers look at and handle merchandise in on-the-ground stores but
then comparison shop and, often, buy on the internet. Moreover, retail
competitors on the internet often have considerably more data on these
customers. Cookies, of course, provide information to any website but
if browsing customers also log into a site (such as Amazon), the firm is
also able to collect browsing information and match it with anything else
it knows about the individual. If you've used such sites, you will know
how they are able to provide targeted recommendations for you, alert
you to new offerings in which you might be interested, and even deliver
timely coupons or other offers as you are on their site. Online merchants
have a huge advantage in terms of personalized marketing relationships,
including customer-specific communications and promotions.

New technology is letting on-the-ground retailers fight back. The same technology has considerable potential in a number of other applications beyond retail, including service industries such as sports or other entertainment providers. Perhaps the best example of a state-of-the-art shopping app incorporating these capabilities is Shopkick.

Shopkick uses geo-location technology to identify users within specific stores. GPS allows this to an extent, but as it is only accurate within tens of meters, a customer could be at a coffee shop down the street when identified as being in a department store. Instead, Shopkick uses Apple iBeacons within stores, sending and receiving communications by way of Bluetooth. If shoppers have installed the Shopkick app, the technology can not only pinpoint what shop they are in within a mall but also what display they might be standing in front of within that store. Based on other data collected by the app at signup and collected on previous shopping behavior, Shopkick adds a "digital, interactive layer" according to a Shopkick executive. Per *eMarketer*: "If consumers use the Shopkick app inside a store, we have their locations, we know their shopping histories and we know their browsing histories."

While a lot of media attention is on how Shopkick can deliver customized communications at the right time (again, much as Amazon can do), the app is also a powerful data collection tool. As noted, background data (demographics and psychographics) are collected when users sign up for the app and download it. The app then collects considerably more data as it tracks the specifics of the user's shopping behavior. Shopkick provides rewards, much like a loyalty card, for certain behaviors. These "kicks" as the rewards are called, accumulate and can be used for goods and services, again much like loyalty card programs. In this case, they are also payback for using the app and allowing it to collect the ultra-precise data. Customers willingly let Shopkick collect and act upon this trove of personalized customer data, on its own and through retail partners. They are paid back with more targeted communications, more targeted offers, and better customer service. In one installation, for example, the Miami Dolphins of the National Football League used Shopkick within their stadium, which enabled them not only to provide an offer on a collectable video card (when fans walked by Dolphin icon Dan Marino's statue) but also to broadcast information on when users should take their seats and where the shortest concession lines could be found.

Part of the message is that with current technologies, unobtrusive data collection is both possible and easy. The amount of data can be considerable.

Again, consider the deep data records that are built and attached to individual, identifiable users. Even if not unobtrusive, users seem willing to turn over even more data if they are provided with some incentive to do it. Shopkick and its retail partners are just beginning to explore the ways such data can be turned into marketing strategies and tactics, but the popular app is indicative of the descriptive research capabilities of modern observation tools.

Kantar

Kantar is one of the largest marketing research firms in the world (and is the parent of Millward Brown, mentioned earlier). One area of expertise they have developed is in social media metrics, "social listening" as they refer to it. Getting a grip on what is happening with social media and the implications for marketers is a new but burgeoning interest for the entire field. Sometimes, getting useful data includes employing new collection and analytics techniques. In describing some of the work Kantar has done, we can get a sense of how descriptive research, especially using large amounts of data, can get a handle on unfamiliar topics such as social media use.

The *2016 Social Media Impact Report* illustrates several different approaches used to study social media behavior in China. Kantar has recruited an online panel of one million who can be sampled for specific research studies. One study, repeated multiple times for a week's duration and with 12–15000 respondents, tracked usage by site, WeChat (messaging) vs. Qzone vs. Weibo (both more social networking), for example, by attitudes toward privacy, and by attitudes toward advertising. Respondents also reported on positive lifestyle influences of social media noting level of agreement with statements like "adjust my mood and relieve pressure of reality" and "make my life more efficient and convenient". Negative lifestyle influences included "lack of privacy protection" and "I sleep less so my health gets worse".

A separate study included 60 cities and sampled 100000 netizens (54000 responded). This study covered usage of social media, penetration by age (participation is going up among older users), trust/credibility of different media (social media is rising), gaming participation (skews young), on-the-ground sports participation, and lifestyle. A similar piece of research, covering 50000 worldwide and over 18000 in China, also looked at usage (times per day and total time) and penetration, as well as top apps. In this case, however, the connection was made between social media and e-commerce use (high relationship in China) vs. social media and entertainment/YouTube (in USA).

Finally, a year-long study examined the top sports and entertainment celebrities in China, constructing a key tracking index. Three hundred celebrities were followed, with data gathered on "buzz volume" or total mentions on the Weibo network. Additional account performance was rated on follower volume, average yearly tweet volume, engagement volume (retweets/comments), and engagement/tweet. The data included 110 million mentions, almost 15000 original posts, 646 million engagements, and over 43000 average engagements per tweet. Key words were also tracked and analyzed with word clouds for each celebrity as were positive and negative emoticons, also added up for each subject.

For a separate study, for a specific client (ITV Media), Kantar looked into the complex issue of multi-screening, examining how viewers interact with several screens (television, mobile, tablet, computer) at the same time. Based on the research, they segmented the market into four parts: social, connected, busy and traditional. "Socials" tend to interact the most with their network, "connected" use online for a variety of things (including some of their television viewing), "busy" are often families who make television viewing an event, and "traditional" are just what they sound like, traditional television consumers. All are growing in their use of devices while watching television, and this research is designed to analyze what that looks like (e.g. social are most likely to be active online during the show, traditionals more likely to be active before and after but not during).

How is that sort of research accomplished? Another study, this one by COG Research for Thinkbox, is illustrative. The research had multiple components, starting with a survey of 1000 people concerning their multi-screening behavior. The results established the level of multi-screening, helped segment the sample by different behaviors, and identified homes of interest for further data-gathering. Twenty households had closed-circuit video cameras installed in their homes for two weeks. A facial recognition software program allowed researchers to identify who was in the room, what screens were on, what show was on the television, and where their attention was focused. Over 700 hours of video were collected, a "digital ethnography" if you remember the terminology from the previous chapter on exploratory research. Fifty households were included in follow-up interviews, including most of the observed sample, to provide deeper insights into their multi-screening behavior.

Given the way we usually frame a research program, this process looks a bit backwards. Usually the recommendation is to gain initial insights from qualitative research and then confirm with quantitative. Here, the behaviors are identified from the quantitative, then confirmed, amplified, and explained by the qualitative. Indeed, the researchers determined that multiscreening actually increased television viewing in the sample. Moreover, when watching television along with other screens, respondents tended to do less channel surfing. When advertising came on, they may have diverted their attention to a device, but they did not change to another channel. Importantly, retention did not change; subjects recalled advertising even if not paying full attention to it. Multi-screening also tended to increase the communal aspect of watching television, increasing connectivity, even if in a different manner.

DISCUSSION #1

Quite a number of prominent characteristics and trends in descriptive research are apparent in these examples. Some are similar to and reinforce things we noticed with exploratory research designs. Some are different. But we can again use them to illustrate and explain how big data and marketing analytics are impacting today's research practices.

Once again, you should notice that the traditional ways we think about descriptive research are still present. Even though in a new context, both the Shopkick data gathering and the Kantar (and related) studies illustrate typical observation research: watching subjects doing something of interest and gathering quantitative data on the behaviors. Shopkick observes behavior within retail stores, a type of study with a long history, even if previously done by an observer physically watching the subjects. Ethnographic observation, as in the multi-screening example, we already discussed in the previous chapter on exploratory research. And, indeed, with only 20 households, this is actually more exploratory in nature even if the amount of video collected is quite sizable. But the technique could easily be replicated on a larger scale with a bigger sample. Observation of activity on social media is newer but, again, fits the template of quantitatively gathering data on consumer activities.

Similarly, surveys are apparent in the social media studies, again collecting easy-to-tabulate responses from a substantial number of people. The thousands of netizens surveyed by Kantar in China are classic communication techniques, carried out on a substantial scale. The preliminary survey of

1000 households by COG Research is also straightforward survey research. The Shopkick example doesn't have a communication component but it should be evident that a questionnaire could be easily executed given their connection to users of the app. They already have contact information, a positive relationship, and a means to reward respondents.

What is newer is the prominence of observation research and a willingness to use both observation and communication to get the job done. We saw the latter case in the exploratory research examples as well. Here, the in-home multi-screening study was predicated on talking to respondents to learn about behaviors, watching them to better understand the details, then talking to them again to get a sense of the reasons for the behavioral details. Similarly, some of the Chinese social media studies observed social media behavior but also communicated with large numbers of respondents about both feelings and behaviors. In cases when an observed individual is known to the researchers and contact information is available (such as Shopkick or a loyalty program member), pairing observation and communication is a simple task.

The prominence of observation research, however, is quite noticeable. It is present in all the examples. And it is present with a large number of subjects. Observation research has existed in descriptive research for quite some time, going back to traffic counts at intersections (for retail location studies) or pedestrian counts on city streets. Originally, such studies needed a human observer to take down the details, so large numbers were difficult and time-consuming. Improvements in technology, such as traffic strips stretched across lanes, made it easier to collect the large quantities of data. The most recent improvements in technology such as the ability to monitor and collect data online and/or ubiquitous video systems have extended the usability of observation studies even further. It's not hard at all to collect reams of data remotely, without a human observer, and often without the respondent even knowing it is happening. Storing and analyzing the resulting database is also fairly straightforward. As a result, observation studies are an increasingly popular and important source of data, sometimes even carried out on a daily or hourly basis.

That ability to constantly collect data on identifiable subjects is related to another trend in the field, the tendency to create panels for research. When an organization constructs a panel, it plans on repeatedly surveying (or observing) members over time. These extended relationships get around the issue of recruiting a new sample every time you want to do research. We'll talk more about them later in this chapter through some specific examples, but note here the possibility of such panels in the Shopkick illustration (and, in fact, any loyalty program is a natural environment for installing ongoing panels) as well as in some of the Kantar research in China.

Much like some of the exploratory work we looked at in the last chapter, contemporary descriptive studies are moving towards more real-world settings and out of artificial data-gathering environments. In the chapter opening vignette, advertising assessment studies were discussed. As noted there, subjects in the past were often exposed to advertising in a movie theater or a research facility. Even if the true purpose was hidden (ad testing depicted as screening a television pilot), respondents knew they were being subjected to something artificial. Today, that may still be true but they will be more comfortable in their own homes as they scrutinize ads at their leisure.

In the other studies we've discussed, the environments are even less artificial. Chinese netizens going about their social media activities wouldn't even know Kantar was studying them in many cases. In others, they may be aware of scrutiny but at least they are in their own world, not under close observation in a testing facility. Similarly with Shopkick, the research takes place in stores with subjects going about their everyday shopping tasks. And just as with some of the examples in the previous chapter, you should be able to see the ease with which "in-the-moment" studies could be done – with contact information and a relationship already in place for potential respondents under observation. The research isn't always unobtrusive, but obtrusive and artificial can be very different from obtrusive and natural or real-world. In the latter case, subjects may even forget about the study over time as they lose themselves in familiar or interesting activities.

Finally, and we've already alluded to this a couple of times in the discussion, collection and analysis tools allow for studies to use very large samples effectively. The automation of data collection allows researchers to observe millions or even hundreds of millions of respondents, as is the case with some of the Kantar social media studies (or a commercial provider like Google Analytics). Even their smaller communication projects in China still had tens of thousands of respondents. Similarly, Shopkick is set up as a service for retailers and a reward program for members but it also effectively collects data everyday on millions of consumers. The resulting databases can be mined immediately for a study at hand or stored until such time as someone in the organization has a question. In either case, the result is an eye-popping amount of data, big data, perfect for marketing analytics.

WHAT'S NEW #2?

Isobar

Isobar, after subsuming Copernicus Marketing, offers an unconscious emotion evaluation system termed Mindsight. As you might recall from a previous chapter, a number of researchers in marketing have developed a growing interest in understanding the emotional responses of consumers, not just their rational processes and responses. That thinking applies not only to exploratory research design but also to descriptive. The challenge in obtaining a true response with descriptive research can be daunting, but Mindsight is one approach to try to accomplish that.

This type of research has several aspects designed to get around the challenge of large-sample, closed-ended data collection on emotions. Initially, emotions need to be understood in context, at a particular point in time or in a decision-making process. They exist only for a short period of time. You might recall one of the approaches to this issue we previously discussed was in-the-moment research, specifically with data collection by mobile. Mindsight uses mobile as its method of administration.

The concept behind the approach also suggests that emotions are something respondents can be reluctant to talk about, especially to an unknown interviewer. Other emotions can be hard to express, even unconsciously, and therefore difficult or impossible to verbalize accurately. The Mindsight approach is based on the idea that pertinent images can produce an emotional response, echoing that which eventually results in rational action. The key is to have the right images and to be able to capture immediate emotional responses.

Mindsight developed and validated a set of images corresponding to nine emotional motivators (security, identity, empowerment, nurturing, etc). Respondents are asked to view images and choose those they associate with their state of mind. From there, analysts can assess the dominant emotions and associate those with the decisions made. Such image-based tasks are easily delivered and choices recorded by mobile devices.

One example illustrates the potential of such an approach. A clothing shopper study was conducted concerning four types of retail outlets: mass merchandisers, club stores, department stores and boutiques. Customers were intercepted within stores by researchers with tablets, given an explanation of the methodology, and left with an instruction card. They were asked to complete tasks on their mobile using the image database within a half-hour.

The project generated 1400 responses and an impressive 80 percent response rate (attributed to respondent interest in the innovative research method). Insights included happy mass merchandiser shoppers feeling responsible about taking care of their families while the unhappy felt trapped and insecure. Emotions varied at the other types of retailers.

Again, the point of the methodology is to hit the respondents with an interesting exercise in-the-moment during or soon after the shopping experience. By doing so and using a variation on projective techniques, researchers are able to obtain a truer response concerning hard-to-express emotions that subjects might be reluctant or unable to provide via a more straightforward technique. Moreover, the approach generates countable responses enabling large sample sizes (and capable of comparison to a much larger set of previous responses, providing some validity in terms of how the answers are interpreted).

Prediction Markets

Prediction markets have been used in a number of settings outside marketing research, especially in circumstances predicting winners and losers (sports betting, political polling). The amount of money or points "bet" on an outcome becomes an indicator of what the public feels will happen. It's polling, but because respondents risk something, be it money or reputation, they tend to favor what they really think will happen rather than what they hope might happen. Again, from a marketing research perspective, you might be able to get behind a façade and find out what they really think.

The technique especially contrasts with concept testing, where a representative sample of targeted consumers are asked about their personal preferences and purchase intentions concerning some new product idea. One prediction market provider, Consensus Point, characterizes this as explicit opinions from potentially uninterested respondents. Alternatively, prediction markets are more diverse samples (beyond the target) and so not representative, but are asked to wager on what other consumers might do. Again according to Consensus Point, tacit judgments from invested respondents. For reasons that the subjects might not even be aware of or may find it hard to explain, they are willing to bet with a certain level of confidence on a specific outcome.

C_space is another research provider running prediction markets. Its methodology is designed to take advantage of a number of strengths of such an approach and to yield accurate predictions for clients, often in the specific sphere of new product success/failure forecasts. The firm uses online communities or panels to provide its predictions, resampling the same group (minus turnover) for different studies.

Respondents are given a set amount of imaginary money and are instructed to bet on one or more of several possible outcomes (for example, which of a group of products will be successful in the marketplace). Participants can choose not to bet at any time, so they tend to put money up only when they have an opinion. This provides some sense of personal investment and confidence to the outcomes on which they do bet. The size of the bets is also an indicator of confidence. The respondent spreading money around to several possibilities has a different story to tell than one who places everything on a particular prediction. Finally, panelists are surveyed after the process and asked to explain the reasoning behind their decisions.

As the market coalesces around an opinion, points are awarded. Those who bet correctly on the market are rewarded, and earlier correct bets are rewarded more highly, as they provide further evidence of the degree of certainty. Typically, the top five point totals receive prizes. C_space has evidence to suggest that the approach allows smaller, non-representative samples to provide equal or better results to traditional surveys. Instead of just reflecting their own preference, respondents provide educated opinions on how the entire market feels. Runs of the prediction markets between different panels (e.g. internal with employees vs. external with consumers) can provide even further insights based on the differing points of view.

Vision Critical

Vision Critical is a research firm that builds "insight communities" for clients, essentially ongoing online panels composed of highly loyal, involved customers. Members are recruited by invitation and actively engaged so as to minimize churn and sustain retention. The client firm is then capable of going out to the community at any time and quickly gathering feedback on just about any question it wants to ask. Consider some examples.

Exterion Media is an outdoor advertising firm based in London, UK. In that type of urban environment, outdoor advertising includes everything from standard billboards to sides of buses and bus stops; subway cars, stations, and tunnels in the Underground; and even sides of buildings. Exterion's insight community is branded work.shop.play and is specifically constructed to include and be attractive to urbanites. The community has over 10 000 members. Exterion seeks "engagement and understanding" of these respondents and uses the community to provide "a regular stream of audience insights".

The instrument format is digital friendly and very visual, allowing subjects to answer questions with swipes and choices among various images. Work. shop.play provides prizes for participation to keep members involved but also recruits new urbanites to keep opinions fresh. The results are used to better understand how respondents feel about outdoor advertising, when it influences them and when it doesn't. As a result, Exterion's sales people are armed with persuasive data when talking to potential advertisers about how and why they buy outdoor media space. Impact on target customers can be quantified.

One example reported an outreach concerning online dating. Exterion quickly found that one-third of single Londoners "wouldn't dream of trying it", 40 percent liked it for its convenience, and those who lived in the capital proper were twice as likely to try it. That and associated data can be of great help in landing and keeping an advertiser in that product category. So Exterion benefits not only from having its own questions answered in a timely fashion but also from being able to complete personalized surveys for its own customers.

Discovery Communications is a global firm with roughly 1.5 billion subscribers for well-known channels such as Discovery, The Learning Channel and Animal Planet. It's "influencer panel" constructed by Vision Critical includes 15 000 members. Discovery executives point out that media companies need to make very quick decisions, that wrong decisions are extremely costly, and so the ability to communicate with viewers anytime is quite important to them. Hence the influencer panel.

Discovery is able to reach out to the community with questions about new products/shows, to gain reactions concerning advertising and promotional campaigns, and to find out about actions of competitors targeting its audience. Techniques used with the panel are again digital friendly, very visual, and meant to be novel and engaging. The firm conducted 120 individual research projects in its first year with the community, giving some idea of the level of interaction (not all members are included in all initiatives).

One aspect of the panels pointed out by Discovery researchers is how ongoing communities lessen the data collection needs of individual surveys. The members have already been vetted, so repeated questions to establish whether they qualify for a particular survey are not necessary. From background data already collected on panel participants, Discovery already knows who fits a sample description or is able to choose those who specifically reflect a desired profile. Similarly, respondents don't need to be bothered with multiple demographic and psychographic questions on each survey, as those data have already been collected. As a result, researchers can get right to the heart of the research and skip the personal details that most respondents don't like answering anyway.

MolsonCoors uses a smaller online community, also constructed with Vision Critical, called the Beer Xchange. Participants are referred to as Beerologists. The panel totals 700 and is segmented by brand but represents a variety of demographics. MolsonCoors researchers refer to the panel as the means to the customer voice, questioning it about products, marketing initiatives, innovation, and other matters. The beerologists are considered "true advocates" who appreciate having their voice heard and especially like seeing their recommendations turned into concrete actions.

MolsonCoors uses the panel for both quantitative and qualitative research. Once again, visually appealing and novel tools are delivered for surveys. And the firm also uses some novel items, including projective techniques such as asking members to keep a diary or write a letter home to a relative. The program delivers "customer intimacy" and also allows MolsonCoors to have an extended geographical reach when seeking feedback.

One important concern with all of these examples should be noted, which is the possibility that the panel of respondents become fanboys of the brand sponsoring the panel, losing their objectivity. Even if that doesn't happen, researchers need to recognize that the panels will tend to be current, satisfied customers, some of the most loyal the firm has. If that is the sample desired, it's fine. But if researchers want opinions from a broader sample, perhaps occasional users or even non-users, the panels won't be appropriate. They have a purpose for which they are very effective, but not all research concerns current customers.

One of the really clear changes in research and analytics in the last decade has been the increased use of ongoing conversations between firms and customers. Some of these take place informally on social media but there has also been a noticeable rise in more structured interactions such as these influence panels. Not having to start from scratch in constructing a sample and gaining respondent cooperation is very attractive to researchers and, as with other innovations we have discussed, there is an ability to collect and analyze greater amounts of data on a more frequent basis than was previously the case. Again, constantly collecting information about customer interactions is a piece of big data. The results can be analyzed immediately for a particular purpose or stored away for combination with other data and deeper analysis at a later time.

DISCUSSION #2

Once again, there are elements of classic descriptive research design in these contemporary approaches. This section has focused more on the communication side of descriptive research, and the illustrations all ask questions of their respondents: How do you feel? What do you think will happen? What is your attitude toward our brand and/or this new product idea? Responses have different forms but most are closed-ended and easily quantified. Large samples are possible with each of these approaches. Further, researchers aren't fishing for new, unexpected insights but rather have relatively well-formed ideas or potential initiatives and are now looking to see the degree of support from their sample. The purposes of the research and general approach remain much the same as those we've always seen in descriptive approaches.

But a number of things are different as well. And there are often good reasons for them, reasons that improve the research in one way or another. In other discussion sections, we've talked about how current techniques often blend observation and communication. That's not the case here. Although observation could be paired with some of these tools, especially community or panel research, not a lot is prominent in these examples. What is fairly clear, however, is the blurring of the lines between exploratory and descriptive research.

Even though large samples are included in each of these cases, there are some examples of open-ended responses. Or, perhaps even more instructive, are the cases where open-ended information has been made more closed-ended, enabling data collection on a large sample level. So in the prediction market case, respondents are asked to explain the reasoning behind their choices: clearly open-ended and would probably be added to the study database as text responses. Panels could be asked anything. Open-ended or closed-ended, the close relationship between researchers and the ongoing panel allows deeper probing and application of just about any technique (recall the projective techniques such as diaries and letters home) which can then be stored and analyzed from any size sample. Finally, the picture-response is specifically designed to draw out deeply held or unexpressed feelings that subjects might otherwise find hard to explain. The results can have the depth of an exploratory study but are collected on the scale of a descriptive one.

The illustrative examples in this section include several other aspects discussed earlier. Longitudinal or repeated measures are possible and even encouraged with influence panels. There are opportunities for in-the-moment data collection, primarily seen in the Mindsight anecdote, but certainly possible with panels. The methods of data collection allow for very large samples, if desired, resulting in big data and, potentially, analytical study. Indeed, as just pointed out, these techniques are capable of collecting unstructured data (text, hard-to-express thoughts) and turning it into big data.

But where these techniques really show an advance over previous research methods is in their relationship with the respondents. As mentioned earlier in this chapter, and as many of you have probably experienced, there are some concerns within the research profession about survey fatigue among consumers. Over-surveying people makes them less likely to respond to survey requests or, when they do, to give the questions their full attention. Telephones as a method of administration began dying, at least in part, because respondents stopped answering their phones or cooperating with research requests. And those who did cooperate were unlikely to be representative of the full population. But there are ways around this problem, and these examples demonstrate several of them.

Initially, having a relationship with the company and/or the interviewer is a big help. When insight panels are formed, the participants usually agree because they like the company and its products. They develop a relationship through repeated interaction and establish even deeper ties as the firm explicitly acts on their recommendations. One major reason consumers decline offers to participate in research is an unknown interviewer or solicitation. That's not a problem with panels.

Even further, these ongoing relationships allow a greater array of reward possibilities, related in some ways to the gamification concept discussed earlier. Incentivizing participation is nothing new, but making it non-trivial and/or interesting is much more motivating than getting a dollar for doing a survey or having a small chance at some larger prize. The prediction market illustration pointed out that those making the earliest correct predictions were rewarded, providing a strong incentive to be invested in the task and to accurately anticipate the opinions of the full sample. In the case of panels, the ongoing relationship can allow respondents to earn points and choices of rewards down the road. From a company whose products they like. There are also psychological rewards, but the point is that there are reasons for participating that just don't exist if someone calls you out of the blue or chases you through the mall with a clipboard.

Hand-in-hand with that aspect of these studies is the notion that these respondents really don't seem to care about anonymity. Traditionally, we worry about guarding the anonymity of subjects, and one reason sometimes put forth about declining to participate is loss of anonymity, whether regarding personal details or being face-to-face with an interviewer. In research where respondents are invested and engaged, they don't seem to be as concerned about anonymity. In the Mindsight studies, consumers have to turn over their mobile contact info and answer some pretty personal questions about emotions and feelings (even if they might not fully grasp what they are revealing). They do so willingly – remember the 80 percent response rate in the clothing shopping study. Similarly, prediction markets need identifiable information in order to reward winners while influence panels have deep background on their participants. The panels also track who is saying what. Again, because of the nature of the relationship, the engaging tasks and the incentives, respondents don't seem to mind.

All of these studies use (or could use) mobile, the method of administration with which respondents are often most comfortable. They also apply interesting, novel approaches. The prediction markets are unique and challenging. The Mindsight images are also something unfamiliar, something that can potentially intrigue even survey-weary participants. Insight panels are often very visual in how they solicit information (from pictures of ten beer bottles with different labels, which do you prefer? From the following six potential advertisements for Shark Week, which is most compelling?), also creating a novel and engaging environment for respondents.

The bottom line is that traditional surveys delivered person-to-person, by phone, or even randomly by digital means are having increasing difficulty in recruiting a representative sample and obtaining fully engaged responses. In order to obtain appropriate amounts of accurate data, especially big data, researchers are becoming more and more creative. The way samples are identified and recruited, the nature of the questions asked, and the method of administration are all areas where a little innovation can yield better results.

STARBUCKS' PUMPKIN SPICE LATTE

Starbucks introduced the Pumpkin Spice Latte (PSL) over ten years ago, looking for another seasonal drink that could duplicate the success of its cold-weather special offerings. Since that time, the PSL has become its most popular seasonal drink ever, selling 16 million cups per year and generating over $80 million every season. The marketing behind the PSL skews heavily toward social media, demonstrating both the data-generating capabilities and the creative marketing that can be done after analyzing the data. Moreover, the innovations can also be seen as a source of even more data, even more precisely segmented.

Louis Rolleigh of SpotRight points out that the product is a good example of how sources of customer data have changed. Where a firm like Starbucks could use loyalty card information to track purchases of PSLs and other products, by customer, those results wouldn't include all buyers. Not everyone has a Starbucks card, especially many of those purchasing a limited-time offering. Commercial offerings, such as transactional data provided by NPD or Nielsen, could also offer some insights and include data on competitive offerings and customers. But much of that is transactional or background personal data. If Starbucks wants data on engagement with the product or something deeper, it would need to do primary survey research. Or take a closer look at social media.

Rolleigh provides a basic yet compelling look at PSL fans by providing details on followers of Starbucks @TheRealPSL Twitter account. They skew younger than the general audience (except for a relatively large percentage of 51–55-year-olds), with young children or teenagers, and are affluent (higher than the comparison group for all incomes above $75 000). They are also decidedly female. In terms of lifestyle, they like celebrity gossip (specifically following perezhilton and peoplemag), cooking (pauladeen and bourdain), and reality television (lots of kardashians). They are relatively less likely to follow fictional characters, health and fitness, or politics (either party), though the interests are still noticeable. In short, "Young, hip, educated, affluent, stable stay at home moms with diverse politics, strong interests in popular culture, health and fitness and preparing their own food" (Rolleigh, 2015).

Beyond the demographics and lifestyle data available, Starbucks' creation of Twitter (113 000 followers) and Instagram (31 000) accounts helps to establish a personality for the brand itself. That aspect allows marketers to track not only changing consumer profiles over time but also brand engagement. The discussions, including topics and sentiments, can be tracked and monitored. Starbucks further stoked interest and customer involvement with social media-based offers such as early availability and "secret" club. The former allows fans to buy the drink before its official launch each year by using the hashtag "#PSLFanPass" and then receive a code to use at their local Starbucks. The Orange Sleeve Society members have their own sub-group with collateral merchandise and membership card. All create interest, some sense of exclusivity, and brand engagement.

What the example highlights is the ubiquity of social media in providing the close relationship and data that can create very high levels of brand loyalty. Marketers have detailed data on their best customers, both general characteristics that can be tracked and identifiable personal information allowing one-on-one communication. Changes in base customer demographics or lifestyle can be monitored over time, as can the level of brand engagement (social media chatter) surrounding PSL. Further, specific marketing initiatives, from launch tactics every year to promotional offers like the FanPass can be tracked as well. All without traditional surveys for data or traditional broadcast media for communications.

PRESCRIPTION FOR DESCRIPTIVE MARKETING ANALYTICS

New developments in big data and marketing analytics enable researchers to reduce survey fatigue while still collecting ever more and ever better data on targeted segments. Marketers can have deeper, more natural conversations with consumers when appropriate but can also obtain considerable data from ongoing observations and communications.

One important lesson is to reiterate that huge amounts of data are already pouring into firms on a regular basis. Much of this tracks routine observation consumer activities, including transactions, web browsing patterns, social media, any other customer interactions, and all sorts of other sources. Once individuals can be uniquely identified by means of things like logins and apps, data can be gathered on them, to be used for analysis in groups or even on that individual basis. Beyond that, organizations can set up regular or one-off projects to collect further observations (e.g.

watching shopping patterns or facial tracking during advertising viewing) or communications (e.g. traditional surveys, panels or prediction markets). Decision-makers have a whole new set of options available for developing understanding of the marketing environment. They can take advantage of any or all of them, but the first step needs to be awareness of what's already available, awareness of the growing use and potential of observation studies, and awareness of the further potential of combinations of observation and communication.

One of the perennial issues in research, especially large sample descriptive research, has always been identifying a cooperative sample and gaining true responses from it. Current techniques have found ways around some of these issues. When data are collected unobtrusively during day-to-day interactions, data tends to come freely given and without any guarding behavior that comes from awareness of being in a research study. When Kantar observes activities of Chinese social media participants or Starbucks assesses emotions behind Twitter postings concerning the PSL, each is essentially recruiting exactly the sample (population in some cases) it wants and gaining full, even enthusiastic participation in the activities on which it seeks information.

When actual samples are required for research, that task can also be more easily accomplished. Many of today's firms already have considerable information on customers as well as contact details. Relationships are already formed. At one end of the spectrum, influence panels can be constructed and employed, being used on as frequent a basis as necessary to fill specific information needs (recall the Discovery average of an outreach every day or two during its first year with a panel). The ongoing relationship provides willing and loyal respondents. At the other end of the spectrum, drawing a new sample can be easier with digital connections as can the ability to reward participants and/or provide them with interesting experiences. The gamification tactics discussed in the previous chapter can be applied to descriptive research as well. Unobtrusiveness, relationships and similar aspects of contemporary research also allow for consistent longitudinal studies, gathering similar data at repeated points in time. Indeed, this is what monitoring systems are all about, but longitudinal studies, always difficult to conduct, have suddenly become not only relatively easy to do but part of day-to-day operations. Marketers can now easily track attitudes and behaviors, specifically looking for trends, inflection points, or other changes in pattern. As with the Kantar social media studies, it's just a matter of taking the time and paying attention to what data are already collected and available for study.

Gamification and related tools also reflect on what can be done with the tasks or instruments themselves. Observations can be performed when participants are doing something more engaging, generating more true responses as they involve themselves in the task rather than reflecting on being research subjects. Similarly, communication approaches can also have more interesting elements, from card sorting to betting on predictions to more interesting visuals for submitting answers. Higher engagement with the research also means the information-gathering process can be as long as needed, particularly in reference to questionnaires. Interesting tasks pull respondents into the survey and motivate them to complete the task. Data gathering, storage and analysis capabilities also allow a wider variety of response patterns. Traditionally, descriptive research leaned towards short-answer questions (and short-form observation results) because large samples were difficult to process if the data were complex. But with current capabilities, even open-ended questions can be included on descriptive surveys. When MolsonCoors wants to use projective techniques such as diaries or letters to home in questionnaires, it can be done. When Starbucks or Kantar want to harvest full text comments from social media, in large quantities, that can be done as well. And those results can be analyzed.

Modern analysis tools can handle these large amounts of descriptive data. The large number of subjects is one aspect but recall that the techniques we've been discussing can also gather huge numbers of variables across each of the subjects, not only describing them and their attitudes or behavior but also the context. Descriptive data are tailor-made for the type of continuous monitoring over time that we talked about regarding big data systems and key performance indicators. Whether shopping baskets and behavior (by segment or even down to specific individuals) or social media activities, all can be continuously gathered, organized and reported. These results can also be studied in more depth with marketing analytics processes. Descriptive data is easily subjected to cross-tabulation, cutting the data by any of the numerous variables collected. If you think about the advertising testing, the results could be cut by any of the accumulated variables, including evidence of smile, frown, surprise, etc. to see the correlations with content or creative executions. Finally, correlations between variables can be identified in a variety of methods we'll discuss, allowing better segmentation and prediction. Specific demographics and card choices in the MindSight case, for example, might predict shopping behaviors and outcomes. Marketers should understand and take advantage of the analytical potential of high volume descriptive data.

BIBLIOGRAPHY

Bain, R. (2010), "Getting the measure of viral ads", available at www.research-live. com, 12 March, accessed 15 September 2014.

Barragan, J. (2014), "Retailers are using mobile apps to drive up sales", *Los Angeles Times*, 28 February, online edition.

Clancy, H. (2014), "Apple's iBeacon signals turning point for mobile engagement", *CNN Money*, 28 February, online edition.

Davies, C. (2016), "Kantar social media impact report 2016", powerpoint deck, available at cn-en.kantar.com/media/1190989/kantar_social_media_impact_report_2016.pdf, accessed 15 September 2016.

Dwoskin, E. and E.M. Rusli (2015), "The technology that unmasks your hidden emotions", *The Wall Street Journal*, 28 January, online edition.

Economist (2013), "Nothing more than feelings", 7 December, online edition.

eMarketer (2016), "How mobile devices close the gap between physical and digital shops", 4 May, available at www.emarketer.com/Article/How-Mobile-Devices-Clo se-Gap-Between-Physical-Digital-Shops/1013912, accessed 15 September2016.

Forbes, D. (2013), "Getting to the truth: How mobile 'in the moment' research is critical to uncovering consumer motivations and experiences", *Alert! Magazine*, 4th quarter, available at www.marketingresearch.org, accessed 15 September 2014.

ITV Media (2016), www.itvmedia.co.uk/research/itv-lives, accessed 15 September 2016.

James, D. (2016), "How the Starbucks Pumpkin Spice Latte became a fall icon", 19 September, available at http://blog.marketing.rakuten.com/affiliate/casual-friday-how-the-starbucks-pumpkin-spice-latte-became-a-fall-icon, accessed 30 October 2016.

McDermott, J. (2014), "Shopkick: Driving retail in exchange for data", *Digiday*, 13 February, available at www.digiday.com, accessed 15 March 2014.

Phillips, T. (2013), "What are you looking at?", 16 December, available at www. research-live.com, accessed 15 February 2014.

Rolleigh, L. (2015), "@TheRealPSL and their real audience", 16 October, available at http://spotright.com/resource/therealpsl-and-their-real-audience/, accessed 30 October 2016.

Schlack, J.W. (2013), "The power of prediction markets", *Quirk's Marketing Research Review*, May, p. 38.

Vision Critical (2016), www.visioncritical.com/customer-stories/exterion-media/, https://www.visioncritical.com/customer-stories/discovery-communications/, https://www.visioncritical.com/customer-stories/molson-coors/, all accessed 15 September 2016.

4

Causal research design

Big data and marketing analytics have also had a huge impact on causal, or experimental, research design. The constant rush of new data into organizations can easily be adapted to experimentation. The result is an off-the-charts increase in testing in some industries and opportunities to constantly tinker with product offerings, pricing, communications, promotional campaigns and other aspects of marketing because of immediate feedback on results. Much like descriptive research, causal designs tend to be quantitative as decision-makers like experimental results that can be demonstrated to be statistically significant. The ease of testing has made quick, qualitative experimental results useful as well, even if not as scalable.

In terms of data, data collection, and analysis, causal research looks much like descriptive research. In fact, the data collected might look identical to much of what we discussed in the previous chapter. Facial tracking to assess reaction to advertising, for example, could be used in either a descriptive or a causal research design. The difference between the two is usually in the conditions of the data gathering. As we'll discuss, descriptive data is collected to describe attitudes, behaviors and so forth. Causal methods will do the same, but look to describe attitudes, behaviors and such in response to a change in some variable. Hence, the experimental design is the key difference, including holding as many variables constant as possible, changing one, and seeing the impact as opposed to just taking in data. If done right, causal research can confirm a hypothesis, providing support that the change in question will actually result in the same outcome in a broader context. If version A of the advertising gains more smiles in facial tracking than does the changed version, version B, it is likely to do so when the ad is actually launched as well.

THE FIRST FIVE SECONDS

Online video as an advertising delivery format has a lot of potential for marketers. With its advent, advertisers saw an opportunity to break free of the 30-second time constraint imposed by other audio/video media. With more freedom, brand stories could be told more fully, perhaps making a more personal connection with current and potential consumers. At the same time, experience has shown that ad-skipping behavior seen in previous media (fast forwarding VCRs or DVDs, channel switching) has followed advertisements to the new platform. Engaging consumers on the smaller screen and convincing them to pay attention throughout an entire ad proved to be a new challenge. With the "skip ad after five seconds" capability built into AdChoice (and an ability to move to other screens during ads without the skip), circumstances raise the question of whether ads should be designed with such behaviors in mind?

Alphabet/Google's YouTube runs thousands of online ads every day and so has a vested interest in understanding consumer viewing behavior. Consequently, the firm has built a database of online ads and their characteristics. Included are ads from 16 countries in 11 content categories. YouTube researchers identified 170 different creative attributes (e.g. brand name mentions, celebrity appearance) which could be attached to individual ads. The researchers could also utilize another Alphabet capability, Google Brand Lift, which measures brand awareness and ad recall to assess the effectiveness of the ads (and, by extension, the creative attributes present in those ads). Google notes success stories like the Mondelez Trident brand in Brazil, helping to determine which cut of an ad to run by finding one version, which resulted in 23 percent higher recall. Or Nissan, discovering that a Canadian campaign particularly resonated with women aged 25–34 and 45–54, guiding them in demographic targeting for the ad.

In studying a number of highly viewed ads, YouTube researchers determined several commonalities. Branding should be carefully done. A blatant brand image early in the video was not a positive unless it was naturally on the product itself. Something to grab attention was necessary to keep the viewer on the ad, including attributes like humor, emotional pull or calming. Smiling people were a positive. And music could be helpful or not. Relaxing or action-oriented music was less effective than something humorous or unexpected. As a prominent success, researchers pointed to the legendary Melbourne Trains "Dumb Ways to Die" ad which although long (three minutes) generated millions and millions of views by being clever, funny and unexpected, along with quirky music and no clue about sponsor until the very end.

Most of that is classic descriptive research, albeit in a very contemporary setting. The Trident example, however, hints at experimentation with different versions of the ad. Note that the same metrics are used as well as the same data collection techniques in descriptive and causal. What's different is how you construct the environment for data collection and analysis. The circumstances determine that the research design is causal/ experimental.

So what does that look like? In this case, a Google team calling itself "unskippable labs" constructed experiments designed to uncover key aspects of online advertising. One experiment reported by the team had to do with a Mountain Dew Kickstart ad "Come Alive", already success-ful on television and online (9 million views in two months). Researchers prepared three cuts of the ad. The first was basically the original 30-second ad with a clear, linear story, quick edits and catchy music. The second was recut to 31 seconds, began with a product visual and countdown to action. The story was less clear but many action shots were similar. The point was to make sure to get the brand noticed before viewers clicked away.

The final version was considerably longer: a 93-second ad with a less explicit brand presentation, less explicit product placement, and a decid-edly less linear story. Instead of starting at the beginning, viewers were dropped into the middle of the action. Intentionally, viewers were given a more cluttered message, requiring them to pay closer attention and view more of the ad in order to make sense of it.

The results of the experiment showed that the longer version generated a 23 percent higher view-through rate (watching the video until the end). The unexpected shifts in the video proved powerful and suggested that viewing may increase on mobile devices when the content is intriguing. In this case, more watched the longer video and those who watched tended to stay for a longer time. Ad recall actually did go down with the longer version but that result did not impact brand awareness, which rose about the same amount for all three versions of the ad. Brand awareness for the longer ad was sig-nificantly higher on mobile devices than on desktops.

The results are interesting and don't solve the "first five seconds" problem. They have suggestions about when and where to brand, how to tell a story, and confirm some of the findings in the more descriptive research. What they do well, however, is illustrate how a causal research design works. We turn to that next.

CAUSAL RESEARCH DESIGN

Causal or experimental research design is specifically targeted at proving a hypothesis. It is the only way to establish causation, or prove that some change will result in some outcome, and so has a very specific role in marketing research. As mentioned earlier, it can often look like descriptive research in terms of sample size, quantitative results, and even the specific variables measured. What is different is the structure of the data gathering.

As with other research designs, causal research can use existing data, observation or communication, though it can be very hard to find existing data after the fact that was gathered in an experimental process. What is more common is to use continuously collected data as a means to measure the results of an experiment, something we'll talk about in some of the examples to come. The major advantage of causal research is that it is the only way to truly establish causation, that changing one thing results in a measurable impact somewhere else. Consequently, this research design has the most reliable results, if done properly. On the downside, it can be the most time-consuming, most costly, and most logistically complex of all the research designs. Experiments can also tip off the competition to possible marketing initiatives to come.

Causal research design is intended as a scientific investigation. The structure is similar to what you might remember from science labs: all but one of some independent variables are controlled, the independent variable of interest is changed, and the impact on a dependent variable is measured. All parts of the marketing mix might be kept constant, for example, except for price. The price (independent variable) is changed, then the impact on sales (dependent variable) is noted. As we'll discuss, there are multiple variations on this design, but those are the basics of a traditional experimental research design.

Structure is important as establishing causation requires several things. Initially, there must be concomitant variation, the independent variable of interest and the dependent variables must both change at around the same time. The larger the time gap, the less likely it is that the former caused the latter to shift. Secondly, the order of change must be right. If sales change first, then price is adjusted, one can't conclude that pricing influenced

Table 4.1   Useful terminology

Causation	Correlation does not establish causation. To "prove" causation, you must demonstrate the following characteristics:	
	Concomitant variation	Variables (independent/predictor, dependent/outcome) must both change at about the same time
	Sequence	The independent variable change should precede the dependent variable change
	Dismiss other explanations	Other potential causes should be eliminated by controlling other variables
Experiments	Internal validity	Experiment in which researcher is able to control variables, isolating the independent variable of interest
	External validity	Experiment in which researcher is able to conduct the test in real-world conditions, increasing confidence that results will also occur if actually implemented
	Laboratory	Experiment done in artificial setting, usually has high internal validity but low external validity
	Field	Experiment done in realistic setting, usually has high external validity but low internal validity
Experimental Design	Refers to the plan of the experiment, especially the sequence of measurements, introduction of experimental (independent) variable, and structure of groups. Many variations, including:	
	Before–after design	Only one group, dependent variable is measured before and after introduction of experimental variable
	Solomon four group design	Two experimental groups, two control groups, two before measures and all measured after introduction of experimental variable
	After-only design	Experimental group, control group, no before measures, but difference in after measures is indicator of change in dependent variable. Simplicity and quality of results make this design very popular in marketing research.
Test Market	New product is introduced in limited market (usually geographically isolated). Full marketing mix is often employed to judge how rollout will work. If successful, full national/international introduction would follow, perhaps with marketing mix tweaked based on results.	

sales. In order to be the cause, the price change must occur first. Finally, the experimenter must be able to dismiss other potential causes. This is why we try to control other independent variables. The more you can isolate the variable of interest, making sure that is the only thing that changes, the more confidence you have in declaring it the cause of any movement in the dependent variable. So you don't want to run a sales promotion at the same time you do the price decrease. If you do, there is no way to determine the individual impact of the two changes, only the total.

This background provides perspective into why the distinction between laboratory and field experiments can be important to the research. A laboratory experiment takes place in an artificial environment. It allows the researcher a great deal of control over all variables (high internal validity) but can be harder to generalize to the real world (low external validity) where those carefully managed conditions probably won't exist. Field experiments take place in the real world and so are very relatable to actual conditions marketers will face (high external validity) but researchers can have a hard time controlling all variables (low internal validity).

What researchers care about in causal research is eliminating potentially biasing factors so as to isolate the true impact of a marketing change. Bias can be internal to the experiment through history (changing conditions), maturation (changes in the respondents), testing effect (measurements tip off the respondents), instrument effect (the instrument for measurement tips off the respondents), mortality (respondents drop out), or selection (improper assignment of respondents to different groups). Externally, changes in place, setting, time or people (essentially anything in the environment) can bias an experiment. So experiments are designed very carefully to change variables and obtain measurements with the least amount of bias.

In traditional marketing research, we often cover different types of experimental designs. We're not going to go into that detail here; that information is easily available elsewhere. But the key point of experimental design choice is to eliminate the biases just mentioned. Building blocks include pre-measurement, post-measurement, experimental groups, and control groups. In order to avoid testing or instrument bias, for example, some designs include groups without pre-measures. But the bottom line is to end up with an ability to measure change (post-measure less pre-measure or experimental group less control group) while designing for minimal bias. There must be a way to do measurements in order to see the impact of the change.

Experimental design has grown so complex over the years that there is growing interest in the field in quasi-experimental design and related structures. Technically, quasi-experimental refers to designs without random assignment of subjects to groups. In practice, you can take it to mean a more relaxed approach to experimentation, especially with large samples in the field. There is sometimes an assumption that one can't control all the variables, so just do a big enough experiment that much of the bias may average out. It's not necessarily scientifically convincing but we'll see that some very interesting results are obtained more from quick, imperfect repeatable experiments done in the field.

Causal research can be done with just about any initiative in the marketing toolkit: the impact of product or packaging changes, price changes, communication changes (or changes in specific communications as in the ad testing discussed above), entry into new markets or new target segments, and on and on. One fairly well-known causal technique is the test market, where firms try out new products (and their full marketing mixes) in a limited geographical market before deciding if and how to introduce them on a fuller scale. We'll discuss those in more detail later in the chapter.

Causal research has a specific but important role in marketing. In circumstances when firms are betting huge amounts of money on marketing choices, decision-makers want as much certainty as possible. Causal techniques are the way to increase that certainty. The connections may not be obvious, but big data and marketing analytics have a great deal to do with how experiments are done in today's world and how they have changed over the past decade or so. Let's look at some examples.

WHAT'S NEW #1?

What's new in the area of causal research? Quite a bit of it has to do with innovations we've already discussed. In areas in which a great deal of data is already collected, especially on a regular basis, experiments come readily to mind. Shopkick could be easily adapted to an experiment in which consumers are offered additional product information, a particular promotion, or a special price on their mobiles while standing in front of the product in a store. Would any of those result in more purchases? Researchers would measure sales before and after the change. Similarly, the Kantar China studies could introduce a new emoticon, a new messaging strategy, or some other social media change to users. Again, what would be the impact on social media responses? All sorts of marketing initiatives could be run by ongoing panels such as those installed by Vision Critical. When data, especially big data, is constantly being gathered, the potential exists for regular experimentation, often unobtrusive. And if the respondent doesn't even know an experiment is happening, the chances of some types of bias, at least, decrease.

LiveAnalytics

LiveAnalytics is a part of Ticketmaster/Live Nation and is the marketing research arm of the entertainment giant. LiveAnalytics has access to the international customer database, Live Insight, including over 60 million consumer records spread across 12 countries. Internally generated data is combined with external demographic data to enhance the depth of the records.

LiveAnalytics UK uses the database to issue targeted reports covering various parts of the UK entertainment scene. UK records include 11 million consumers with data collected from 46 million transactions. Researchers drew on this customer data, for example, for their report on the UK theater industry. That particular study focused on recent attendees (at least one theater event in the previous three years), mainly from the UK (1006 respondents) though with roughly 500 respondents from other countries for perspective. Although some data in the study could be pulled from the observational database, other data came from an online survey. The survey included both closed-ended and open-ended response patterns.

The results had some predictable results such as most represented age range (25–34 and 35–44) and a female skew as well as some less expected ("social" attendance by groups and teenagers had the strongest intention to attend in the future). Topics covered included appropriate behavior at the theater (mobile phones?), barriers to attendance, sources of information concerning performances, and average spend (including but going beyond just tickets). Comments on everything from the immersive nature of the theater experience to positive impressions of interactivity and receptivity toward loyalty programs provided insights for future marketing initiatives.

This *"State of Play"* report is clearly descriptive research conducted with the aid of a big data database the firm has built over the years. Though the events that Ticketmaster/Live Nation manage are on-the-ground, most of their transactions are online, allowing them to track interactions with customers. The tickets themselves, when scanned, are joined to each individual's record. Further, since the customers are identifiable, they can deepen profiles by adding external data on each individual, including demographics and, presumably, lifestyle details.

But the database, combined with processing and analytical capabilities, allows LiveAnalytics to do even more. Personalized marketing can be done, in much the way that online retailers and service firms make recommendations or steer marketing communications to individuals. With analytics, for example, researchers were able to determine that attendees for a particular comedian were not likely to attend a particular second comedian's show (as standard marketing might suggest) but in fact were 163 percent more likely than the general public to attend an offbeat comedic play ("Jumpy") then showing in London's West End.

The team's process is broken down as: data, analysis, insight and action. With an emphasis on action, the research function not only enhances planning for future initiatives but also optimizing current ticket sales, better enabling Ticketmaster and its clients. And, more to the point of this chapter, it also enables experimentation.

One common challenge with live events is ticket prices. Too high a price and too little in sales is an obvious problem, but too low a price and high sales tends to leave money on the table (attendees would have paid more) and encourages scalping behavior. Scalping not only opens up an unauthorized channel but also brings fraud, fake tickets and other matters into the mix, with the potential for customer dissatisfaction issues and related poor word-of-mouth.

LiveAnalytics has been able to conduct in-the-moment experimentation related to ticket prices. In particular, during a recent Kid Rock tour, pricing was adjusted for the best seats in relation to what was going on with supply and demand. Initially, more shows were scheduled than were typical for such a tour, ensuring that supply for some seats was readily available. Kid Rock and Ticketmaster marketers then monitored the supply and price of tickets on secondary markets (scalpers), adjusting the price of their own top tickets in relation. Essentially immediate experimentation, the nature of the industry allows Ticketmaster to adjust prices on the fly (the independent variable) and observe the impact on sales (dependent variable) as well as on supply/price on the secondary market (a second metric that impacts sales).

What is interesting about the experiments, and others that LiveAnalytics can run, is not only the real-world aspect and ability to change variables dynamically. But the millions of consumers with whom Ticketmaster has a database relationship allow it to reach out to almost the entire population of potential ticket buyers when conducting such experiments. Sampling is less an issue than the ability to communicate with an entire consumer population, making changes to the marketing proposition as conditions dictate.

Decision Insight

Decision Insight is a research provider known for its virtual shopping capabilities. The firm is able to introduce respondents to a realistic retail setting, with both three-dimensional (store layout) and two-dimensional (shelves) elements. Traditional test markets use actual stores, introducing a new product to the shelves, supported by the marketing communications intended for the launch and monitored for sales results. Beyond on-the-ground traditional tests, test markets in laboratories developed as a way to control all variables of the experiment (including competitor reactions, for example, such as price changes, promotional campaigns, etc.). Some of the laboratories were also on-the-ground, physical facilities made up to represent a store with shoppers instructed to choose items as if for real. With advancing technology, virtual facilities became another way to control all variables while shoppers interacted with the artificial environment. Further, virtual shopping allowed researchers to immediately change variables of interest while also collecting and processing data in real time. Without the need of recruiting actual shoppers to be physically present, virtual shopping can also be much quicker and provide a more geographically diverse sample.

Decision Insight's ShopperIQ system is a virtual shopping system allowing clients to experiment with different retail environments, including aisle creation (product categories included), assortment (what items within a brand or brands), arrangement (what goes where on the shelves), merchandising (presentation of items, including displays), pricing and packaging. All can be changed and presented to respondents quickly, allowing tests to change mid-stream as additional data comes in.

More recently, researchers have been able to add advanced technologies such as eye tracking. Such tools allow feedback not only on product choices but also on what parts of the shelf or package the respondents focus on (and for how long). Decision Insight also has the ability to add communication to the process, questioning respondents about the attitudes and motivations behind the shopping decisions.

One of Decision Insight's options is termed the Consumer Decision Tree and focuses on how, specifically in what order, respondents make purchase decisions. Although the decision-making process is a long-standing topic in consumer behavior, researchers traditionally collect information on it by means of focus groups or panels, as we've discussed previously. Here, researchers allow respondents to react to virtual store representations, quantitative results reflect decisions made, while qualitative sheds light on the reasons why. In one example, Decision Insight was able to determine that consumers chose form (the product type) before moving on to choose brand. Such conclusions help with arranging aisles by product/form with multiple brands rather than grouping first by brand. Further, researchers were able to identify a segment of high-income, more sophisticated consumers with slightly different decision processes for whom the retail experience could be further adjusted for good effect.

Once decision processes are clear, options for addressing them can be tested, bringing forward more experimental approaches. For aisle flow, for example, the virtual shopping program can adjust where products and categories (sub-groups of the products by their definition) are slotted, what products are adjacent to what other products, and what categories are near what other categories. Different options can be tested by respondent shopping choices, eventually settling on the optimal way to set up the items on the shelves. In one test, children's multi-vitamins did well slotted next to adult multi-vitamins, and joint health products performed well beside menopausal remedies. There was no previous evidence that the two groups needed to be anywhere close to one another. Further, calcium supplements and pre-natal vitamins also demonstrated a strong link to menopausal remedies, showing good results when adjacent.

From there, additional experimentation can determine what assortments and arrangements work best. Which brand, which size, which specific item (stock-keeping unit or SKU), at what price in each location can be tested. The example provided by Decision Insight is a major salty snack provider testing the difference between a checkerboard arrangement (national brands and store brands intermixed) vs. a shopper arrangement (choices arranged by shopper needs, e.g. price-sensitive vs. brand-loyal) and finding the latter to generate more profit from the aisle.

Again, what all of these offerings and examples have in common is a data-based approach to store set-up determined by experimentation. In terms of the template presented earlier, it should be clear that the tools offered by Decision Insight allow researchers to present layouts to respondents. These contain numerous variables that can be manipulated, including aisle flow, arrangement, pricing and the others noted. In classical experimental design, all but a single variable can be held constant to isolate the impact of a specific change (e.g. price decrease or shelf position). An aisle arrangement can be set, for example, along with assortment and pricing. A new package design can then be inserted into the display, and researchers can track whether consumer choice of that item goes up or down significantly. With no other change in environment apparent, the change in potential sales can be attributed solely to the package design adjustment.

With contemporary technology, we can do some more complex things with experimental design, manipulating variables in a way that allows more testing but still in a way to isolate the ones of interest. Further, researchers can bring in additional data-gathering tools such as eye tracking or qualitative techniques including ethnography. All in all, the approaches add up to a much quicker, less costly, and fuller picture of how a change in the shopping environment (including a new product introduction) will impact market share and profitability.

DISCUSSION #1

In these newer approaches to causal research design, we see some patterns similar to the trends found in exploratory and descriptive research design. As in those cases, multiple approaches and techniques are often combined to good effect, amplifying strengths while minimizing weaknesses of any particular tool used in isolation. Similarly, the lines between what is exploratory and qualitative vs. descriptive or causal and quantitative are clearly starting to blur.

In particular, one can see in the LiveAnalytics example an ability to collect large-scale quantitative data on ticket purchases and reactions to experiments such as price changes and personalized communications or promotional offers. But at the same time, researchers are able to reach out to identifiable respondents for additional qualitative information concerning the attitudes and motivations behind these observed quantitative behaviors. In the case of Decision Insight, experiments can be done and quantitative data collected easily by means of the retail simulations. But, once again, there is a mechanism to look for deeper insights by communicating with subjects directly on the reasoning behind their decisions as well as further explorations on what they particularly noticed about the brand, package, shelf position and so on vs. competitor attributes. Indeed, in studies adding a real-world retail store environment, Decision Insight now also offers a mobile, in-the-moment component to allow it to gather immediate communication feedback, much like some of the exploratory and descriptive research providers we have already looked at.

Both of these examples and the potential blending of research designs, techniques and data types also illustrate the trend we've noted multiple times throughout this book: the combination of observation and communication approaches. Although not used in all studies, both groups of researchers clearly have the ability to do both observation and communication. From observation, as we know, they can see actual behavior. In one case it's an artificial environment (virtual shopping) and in the other it's in the real world (event ticketing), but the result has the advantage of being true to life, individuals acting in response to whatever stimulus the researchers provide. But, as you know, while behavior observation does provide a truer indication of how respondents will act, it doesn't provide the thought process behind the action. That can only be gathered with communication. That can be done here, and, more importantly, a specific thought process can be tied to a specific action of identifiable individuals.

Part of this has to do with ongoing relationships established with participants. We've already discussed this trend regarding influence panels, registered users, and other continuing partnerships. That's certainly apparent in these examples, particularly in the case of LiveAnalytics. Even though not organized as research panels, the firm does have continuous contact with the individuals in its database. And although apparently not a loyalty program, it does have the elements of deep demographic and behavioral profiles typical of such initiatives. This allows continuous contact with known and well-understood customers. It also allows real-world, field experiments targeted to specific customer groups (e.g. 25–34-year-old females who attended live musical theater in the last six months) with built-in data-gathering capabilities. The subjects can be conditioned to periodic communications so that communications and measurements become routine and unobtrusive.

The use of current technology to gather huge amounts of data is also apparent. As already noted, LiveAnalytics has a massive customer database in the tens of millions combined with additional detail on the identifiable individuals within that database. It collects the transactional data itself through its regular operations, and this can be supplemented with any communications, by any medium, with its customers. The database can be monitored for changes and trends (as well as post-measurements for experiments) or looked at more deeply with analytics tools.

Decision Insight's virtual shopping platform can also take advantage of technological capabilities to gather data. The online nature of the simulation feeds consumer reactions directly into its databases, supplemented with any background information the firm has assembled. As noted earlier, these data can include metrics such as eye-tracking, mobile interviews, and other data. All in all, these approaches can also be connected to individuals (if respondents are reused) or specific variable manipulations, again enabling the type of marketing analytics that can discover patterns and combinations in big data sets.

Specific to causal research, the really interesting part of these approaches is how they can help to minimize some of the common biases in experiments. We noted a number of internal biases within experimental designs earlier, and there are always the possibilities of things happening in the wider external environment (everything from rain to a distracting news event to competitor activities) that can push results in a particular direction not representing true feelings or behaviors. On the one hand, we have more unobtrusive techniques, as with LiveAnalytics, where respondents would probably not even know an experiment is occurring. On the other, as with Decision Insight, we have engaging stimuli, with the actual manipulations somewhat hidden, that can again make the fact that an experiment is happening less than top-of-mind. Both tend to decrease the risk of internal biases.

The case of LiveAnalytics is easy to see. Anytime there is an ongoing relationship with a brand, with frequent communication and regular transactions, researchers can gather new data unobtrusively. This is particularly easy with loyalty programs but any organization with continuous interaction with identifiable customers can do similar things. Gathering data on customer preferences, customer choices, or how they respond to specific communications, price changes or other offers can build a deep database on behaviors and context. The constant opportunities to measure or collect data on attitudes and behaviors makes any specific outreach seem routine. Experimenting with a price change or a promotional offer is just part of the relationship. When the subjects of the experiment don't even realize it's going on, there is much less chance of things like instrument bias, testing bias, and so forth getting in the way. Doing the experiment on a wide basis, in the real world, can help with some of the external biases. Researchers hope that any specific bias (e.g. raining in Poughkeepsie) might be washed out by a range of other occurrences (not raining in Peoria). One can't control the real world, but having a wide scope to the experiment or repeating it can lead to some of the external biases evening out, yet another attractive aspect of big data.

LiveAnalytics tends to use field experiments, helping with the unobtrusiveness and some bias minimization. What about Decision Insight? In this case, at least in front of a screen with a virtual store aisle, the respondent clearly knows research of some kind is happening. The simulation is a classic laboratory experiment with its artificial environment. What is particularly interesting about the Decision Insight approach is the engagement level. The virtual shopping exercise has unique, innovative visuals, almost a gamification of the shopping process. If the technology and approach are intriguing enough for the respondent, the artificiality of the setting and obtrusiveness of the research aren't as top-of-mind. If subjects lose themselves in the task, the potential internal biases are less likely to be a problem. The laboratory setting itself can minimize external biases even though external validity can still be an issue (transferring lab results to real-world settings, though Decision Insight claims to have 90 percent reliability in such matters). The point is that current technology can not only make the data gathering and processing quick and easy but can also make the tasks more engaging, allowing more data collection and potentially less biased data collection.

WHAT'S NEW #2?

Dynamic Pricing

Dynamic pricing is a marketing tactic long practiced by airlines and other service providers who have limited capacity and variable demand. Also referred to as yield management, providers vary prices according to conditions. If many seats on a given flight are still available close to scheduled takeoff, prices will fall. If few are available but high demand is anticipated, prices will rise. Mismatches of supply and demand will trigger price changes.

One observed trend in the big data economy is an ability and willingness of some e-tailers to try dynamic pricing in other conditions, in different circumstances. Indeed, some on-the-ground retailers are also finding ways to adjust pricing rapidly in the wake of new information. Prices can change regularly for some offerings, as well as some other parts of the marketing mix (e.g. promotional offers), once decision-makers get a handle on which changes can make a difference in optimizing the price/demand dynamic.

Observers have tested online retailers and other service providers regarding prices for specific products. Staples, for example, priced a brand-name stapler at $15.79 for one e-shopper and at $14.29 for another a few miles away. Cheaptickets and Orbitz have been observed offering higher price quotes to visitors not logged into their sites. Travelocity was found to be charging browsers using Apple's iOS 15 percent more than those using a different operating system. Home Depot was seen to direct mobile users to more expensive products ($100 higher) during some searches than it did personal computer users.

Such tactics are relatively simple in the online environment where sign-ins, cookies and browsing histories provide sites with extensive data on users (and price changes or other reactions are easy). But they are moving to on-the-ground environments as well. Kohl's can vary prices throughout its stores since going to an electronic pricing system. The Indianapolis Zoo installed dynamic pricing, ranging from $8 to $20 for admission based on advance sales and expected demand. Highway tolls can be varied depending on volume, as can ski resort tickets. Similar actions are taken by providers such as Uber, Lyft and Disney. In such cases, revenue or profit maximization isn't necessarily the only objective as providers may also aim to shift demand (move high volume from busy periods to slow periods).

A more specialized application of dynamic pricing is seen with online merchants selling through other platforms. On Amazon, for example, multiple merchants often sell the same item through the parent site. In that case, having the most attractive price when a customer searches for a product leads to having the most prominent position in the results, in the "buy box" as it's called. Data shows that 95 percent of consumers tend to pick the buy box, so landing there is critical. Consequently, such merchants change prices frequently and, at times, dramatically. During one 24-hour period, a microwave oven was tracked on Amazon and ranged between $744.46 and $871.49. Based on other observed variables, the pattern appeared to respond to competitor prices, competitor shipping charges, manufacturer price constraints, and seasonal sales patterns. The merchants had developed an algorithm to respond automatically to changes in such variables with additional settings built in to provide some controls on frequency of price changes, which competitive prices to track and to which to respond, and which competitive prices to ignore.

These changes in price, specific product or features offered, or other tweaks to the marketing mix are not experiments themselves, they are straightforward marketing tactics. But in order to decide what tweaks to make, decision-makers have undoubtedly done considerable experimentation. The ability to change these marketing mix variables immediately and across the entire population of buyers allows real-world experimentation on a level we really haven't seen before. And the experimentation can be very complex. How did a vendor decide on $744.46 for the rock bottom price offered on the microwave at certain times of day? Probably by trying out $744.40, $744.41 ... $744.49, $744.50, and all over the scale to see which option generated the optimal blend of low enough to find the buy box while still high enough to generate profit. Similarly, varying time of day, perhaps the specific item (different versions might have different features), and other inputs such as shipping prices, decision-makers can optimize all aspects of the offering through highly structured, complicated experimental designs. Although external variables can't be controlled, the sheer size of the experiment (basically, the entire population of customers and potential customers) creates the assumption that biases should even out. Internal variables, of course, are tightly controlled. One of the most critical aspects is that the experimentation is done in the real world and results constantly updated, so the conclusions are fairly trustworthy. Another interesting aspect is that competitor reactions don't stay stable either, so experiments need to take place continuously to keep up with changing conditions.

Changing prices in this manner is a form of A/B Testing, used to compare two versions of a web page (web page A vs. web page B). As noted, the marketer is able to adjust any number of internal variables while controlling the rest. Aspects of web page appearance including headlines, images, text, action buttons, links, and other pieces can be adjusted, as can marketing initiatives such as pricing, promotions, additional services (shipping and delivery) and so on. Visitors are assigned to one version or the other of the web page. Metrics that can be used to assess the differences between the versions include traffic, time spent on the page, and conversions. The last, obviously, is the key to determining what a dynamic pricing program might look like.

A/B testing is often associated with the visual presentation of the web page though, as noted, differences in content (text, price, promotion) and its appearance can be tested in the same manner. To illustrate the process, consider an experiment done for AMD by Wingify with its Visual Website Optimizer. Placement of the "share this" panel with its "chicklet" buttons leading to different social media was tested. Different locations (bottom, right, left) and chicklet sizes (large, small) were tried, six different options. The versions staying anchored on the sides (always visible, despite scrolling) generated substantially more sharing (36 times more!) than the versions on the bottom (though some changes were also made to a software driver which probably also had some impact).

Real-world, real-time testing and adjustment is possible with enhanced technology, data storage and data processing, the aspects of big data and marketing analytics we have been discussing. Moreover, while formal experimentation can easily be done, as per A/B testing and related techniques, marketers can continue to adjust prices and other variables as they continue to make changes and see results. Experiments can take place all the time, as part of the everyday experience of customers. Essentially, today's world offers the prospect of continuous causal research, amplifying its ability to deliver useful real-world insights when and where needed.

Loyalty Programs and Beyond

The sorts of pricing and other adjustments noted in the previous section generate enormous amounts of data and enable deep analytical study on a regular basis. The techniques are typical of experiments aimed at the entire targeted segment. Different versions of web pages or other means of presenting the variations are offered to individuals within the segment, usually randomly, and their reactions are measured and evaluated as a group. Actionable insights are then executed toward groups with similar tendencies.

But we can go even deeper with advanced capabilities. In particular, causal research can now be tied to individual customers. Given the ability of marketers, both online and offline, to make personalized offers to customers on whom they already possess considerable background data (including demographics, psychographics, browsing patterns and transaction histories), experimentation to increase the customer's value is the next logical step. Anyone who has bought from Amazon knows its capabilities in terms of offering personalized recommendations, offers, new product alerts, and other such custom communications. While not always perfect, these can again get better over time as more data are collected.

Earlier in the book, we discussed the pioneering efforts of some loyalty program innovators, including Tesco and Harrah's/Caesar's. One of the drivers of big data and marketing analytics is the huge amount of data that can be collected by such programs. Even larger databases result when loyalty program data is paired with that from other sources. From the databases, with individually identified members or customers, marketers can do experiments. Importantly, there is a capability of experimenting on individuals and, again, they are not anonymous; the key is identifying how to connect better with each identifiable individual. Caesar's, for example, with their Total Rewards program, is able to monitor individual behavior and make different promotional offerings to card members. If the customer hasn't been to a property in an unusually long time, what can be done to reinstitute the previous behavior? Or if the goal is more frequent trips to casinos or resorts, the firm can experiment with different offers, assessing which do the best job of attracting that specific customer to return. Do they respond to an offer of a free room? To an offer of a free show? To an offer of a free meal? To an offer of money for gambling? Essentially, the organization is able to manipulate promotional variables until it finds something that works. It can then continue experimenting to optimize the revenue/promotional spending relationship.

While the objective with Total Rewards members is to increase the number of stays and cross-sell additional offerings, Caesar's also has a strategy for what it calls frequent independent travelers (FITs). FITs are more promiscuous in terms of their destination choices. They average one stay per year at Caesar's properties as opposed to three stays per year for Total Rewards members. The objective with FITs is not just to increase stays but to convert them to membership. Even without the deep data files on these individuals, Caesar's is still able to identify them when they interact with its websites, tracking their activity, assessing the impact of social media, and doing A/B tests for different website displays. As with its loyalty program members, experimentation can be done down to the individual level. In one test, for example, site visitors looking for a reservation were sent randomly to the main Caesar's site or to the website of a specific property. While more rooms and other services weren't necessarily sold, the latter group did sign up for Total Rewards at a significantly higher rate.

As noted, this is very similar to what Amazon does, though Caesar's doesn't necessarily need to be online, at least when dealing with loyalty program members. Amazon will also vary messages (new video streaming options, new romantic fiction from a favorite author, an electronic device with new features, etc.) and offers (a sale, free shipping, a branded credit card, etc.) with the objective of increasing the value of each customer, the lifetime customer value, through more frequent and/or larger purchases.

Once again, there is a deep, personalized database representing anyone with an Amazon account, especially those enrolled in Amazon Prime.

One might note that we have been talking almost exclusively about retailers or other service providers with direct connections to end consumers. Manufacturers and other organizations without the direct consumer relationship have been envious of this close relationship and the ability to gather data and/or experiment with actual customers. Hence, a newer trend is for consumer goods providers to try and establish these connections themselves. Procter & Gamble (P&G), for example, did have some direct relationships with consumers but these were often disjointed, depending on product or market, and not as analyzable as they could be. Consequently, P&G created "1, Consumer Place", a data platform bringing together all of its 4.8 billion worldwide consumers in all markets and for all products.

The key capabilities of the database are highlighted in that last sentence. Individual consumers could be identified across product categories. The example often provided is the Pampers diaper buyer who often has a close relationship with P&G while children are young but eventually grows out of the category. Previously, P&G might have lost the relationship but the new platform allows them to continue to link with the consumer, particularly in related categories such as health and beauty or household cleaning products. The longer relationship and centralized data allow a better understanding of each consumer, including individual preferences concerning products, communication channels (especially digital) and promotions. Once again, experimental techniques including A/B tests can be applied, both by segment and by individual. Finally, lessons learned through experiments in one market can help guide decisions (and further experiments) in other markets. If a marketing offering is optimized in China, for example, transferring those learnings to other parts of the world can be useful, as can additional tests to further customize the offering to other markets. All in all, the objective is personalized data on all 4.8 billion consumers and an ability to individualize offerings across the marketing mix to every one of them. The method is big data, analytics and experimentation.

DISCUSSION #2

Standard experimental design, or at least the possibilities for complex designs, should be obvious from this discussion. Again, the basics of causal research haven't changed, even with new approaches. But, at the same time, current capabilities in data collection and analysis have opened up amazing new vistas for marketing research. In terms of traditional experiments, the examples noted provide a structure with controlled variables (a number of aspects of the marketing offering that are held constant), a manipulated variable (price, web page content/design/details), and metrics to judge impact (before/after measures, experimental group/ control group measures). The designs can sometimes be very complex, with numerous experimental variables each manipulated in turn, in part because of the ease of conducting the test and the size of the sample or even entire population available.

Which brings us to some of the important changes that have occurred over the past decade. Initially, as noted throughout this text, the presence of big data and business analytics is ubiquitous, allowing marketers to mine those large populations for experiments. To do a test such as the AMD chicklets experiment mentioned earlier, one needs six distinct experimental groups, one for each version of the web page. In order to have statistically reliable results, that demands a fairly large sample, one that might be difficult to recruit in a more typical in-person setting. And, as we've noted, the experiments can get much more complex, with many more experimental groups as the number of variables and their permutations grow. What's really interesting about some of the experiments done in a big data context is that samples aren't even involved. Changes (such as dynamic pricing) can be rolled out to the entire population to see what happens. When the entire population has been tested, statistical reliability becomes an afterthought. The sample doesn't need to be extended to the population; the population itself can be subjected to experimentation. That's a new and very different development. The excitement it provides statistics geeks may be difficult to understand, but it eliminates the possibility of sample biases and extending results beyond the sample. The results, by definition, apply to the entire population of users, customers or whoever might be included.

Another characteristic of big data we've repeatedly mentioned is its unstructured nature, the ability of contemporary systems to take in all sorts of data inputs (text, video, images, etc.) for storage and analysis. These experimentation techniques also take advantage of this capability, both in the ability to manipulate variables and, especially, in measuring impact. Changing the appearance of web pages, changing prices in real time, customizing offers to individual customers isn't really about collection of unstructured data but these techniques do illustrate an ability to roll out a variety of options to subjects in real time. The data capabilities behind such changes, being able to keep them organized and trackable and then taking in resulting data (and keeping that organized and trackable) all illustrate the power of modern information technology that can be trained on data collection and marketing analytics.

But the ability to capture unstructured data as a metric for experimental results is potentially an even bigger step forward. Based on a change in any of the variables we have discussed (pricing, promotional offerings, web page presentation), researchers can monitor impact through measures such as customer inquiries/comments, social media chatter, image/video postings on social media, and any number of others, including new channels we may not even have seen. The positive or negative impact of changes can be measured, not just by spending, but by more innovative metrics that may better indicate consumer engagement and brand experience. We can actually track consumer sentiment now, not just consumer purchasing.

As mentioned in other discussions before this one, the nature of big data and recurring points of contact with consumers also provide opportunities for longitudinal data collection, so the impact of variable changes can be measured over time. This can lead to some really interesting, really complex experiments as the testing can have several components, adjusted over time. An initial change can be assessed, then further tested and optimized as time goes by. This can be particularly important for pricing experiments. As noted, one can get an idea of an ideal price for a segment but then can actually vary it by smaller and smaller increments to determine the absolute best price. The same could conceivably be done for individuals, adjusting the marketing variables to maximize customer value. So Caesar's, for example, can track not only the variable that draws in the specific loyalty program member but, through additional testing, exactly what value should be assigned to that variable (e.g. offering a room at reduced cost and then optimizing exactly how much the reduction should be for each member). Moreover, the price optimization can continue to be tracked so that when the inevitable competitor reactions occur, the price can be re-tested and re-adjusted, continuing to optimize given changes in conditions.

Also to be noted is the tendency, once again, toward observation research. Although communication is possible and even encouraged by the close relationship between the organizations and their members and identified users, these experiments largely depend on observation of consumer behavior in response to marketing prompts. What do consumers do after a change in price? How do consumers react based on differences between websites? Which promotional offer gains a higher level of consumer response? As noted, communication can be added as well, particularly when looking for an explanation of why the behaviors took place. But the heavy observational component is again obvious.

As we have already discussed, observation studies can often be done less obtrusively than communication and will tend to show how subjects really act rather than how they say they might. In these cases, where bias is such a concern, unobtrusiveness is a major advantage. If individuals don't know an experiment is being conducted, their responses can't be influenced. Hand in hand with this perspective is the interesting way in which these types of experiments can employ the best characteristics of both field and laboratory experiments. As noted earlier, lab experiments have the advantage of variable control; the conditions of the test can be carefully held constant or changed. Field experiments have the advantage of real-world conditions, more like what might actually happen after the test is over. Here, the researchers are able to conduct their experiments in the real world (field experiments) but with the advantage of control over many of the variables (lab experiments). There can still be issues with external conditions, of course, that are beyond control such as events in the economy, politics, the weather or elsewhere. And competitor reactions remain beyond control, of course, though frequent experimentation and other changes in marketing offerings can still hide when true tests are occurring (lessening the probability of a competitor noticing and taking actions to spoil the results). All in all, the ability to hide that an experiment might be taking place, from both subjects and competitors, has been dramatically enhanced.

Contemporary experimentation is often quick, easy and inexpensive. And it can generate even better, more unbiased results than a number of traditional methods of testing. Some firms experiment so much that the attempts are ubiquitous and, being ubiquitous, are virtually unnoticed by subjects. The results can be compelling and reliable.

GAME TESTING

Much like test markets for consumer packaged goods, software-driven products are often rigorously tested before a final version is introduced. This can include computer software such as operating systems or programs for office and creative tasks, mobile apps, or gaming systems. Games, in particular, often follow a pattern of usability tests, with select subjects trying out the game at an early stage, followed by alpha and beta testing. Alpha provides a nearly ready-for-market game to players inside the firm, asking for feedback on the experience. Beta does the same, but for players outside the firm, usually current or potential customers. At this stage, the testing has usually been about identifying bugs and other issues with the game before it is introduced to the world.

Traditionally, both usability and beta testing was done by providing respondents with a copy of the game, having them play it and then return some instrument with comments. These instruments could be quantitative or qualitative, with closed-ended questions for specific things developers want feedback about and open-ended questions for describing anything unanticipated or to get an in-depth impression of the game from players. In today's world, however, games are increasingly played on the internet or at least connected to it, allowing researchers to collect game playing data as it happens. That capability has dramatically changed how beta testing is done, both in terms of the sample size and the nature and amount of data collected.

Kenneth Hullett and his colleagues reported on several examples of contemporary beta testing for games, including one specific offering with which they were involved for the XBox 360. With the new capabilities for beta tests, developers continued to focus on finding bugs but also started to collect other data designed to improve game play. Some of this involved the activity in the game, so one study tracked player deaths in one of the *Halo* updates while also asking subjects their opinions on the difficulty level, allowing designers to avoid unintended jumps in difficulty. Another tracked 5000 game plays of *World of Warcraft*, looking for indicators of strategy from subjects. These results were used to create an algorithm for the playing bot that could anticipate and counter those strategies. Games were also adjusted in terms of levels and designs based on this type of big data feedback.

Beyond play testing, researchers were also able to use tools such as eye tracking to see where user attention was focused on the screen (helping to place clues more effectively within the game) or to see where players' eyes were drawn given different interface designs. Another *Halo* version included a beta test with 2.7 million players totaling 16 million hours of gaming. This allowed not only identification of bugs but also game adjustments for minute factors such as weapon damage, reload times and recharge times.

The specific beta test covered by Hullett et al. included thousands of subjects and 3.1 million game plays. Data were collected concerning the game play and the users' background, particularly their gaming history. The specific results reported included the game mode (online/offline/single player, etc.), game event (e.g. street race, test track), and choice of vehicle. The low usage of some of the 134 available vehicles as well as game modes and events allowed some trimming as each individual design requires considerable time and attention from highly paid creators and artists.

You should be able to see a number of the elements we've been discussing in terms of experimentation in these examples. As this is real-world causal research, there are lots of moving parts and no explicit effort to fully control the environment of the testing. But the large sample sizes in several cases provide some confidence of the reliability of the eventual results. The beta tests are classical experiments in terms of before/after measurements or control groups, and the experimental variable is essentially the beta version of the game with lots of smaller pieces also to be measured. But the general idea of putting the product out there prior to launch to gather data to help optimize the product and its marketing fits very well with the concept of causal research. The test market approach, putting a new offering into a limited market and then tracking impact, is very much in line with what causal/experimental research design is intended to do. The influence of big data is seen in the ease, speed and expanded measurements that can be brought to the testing as well as being able to use objective observational data to supplement or replace the more subjective communication approaches.

PRESCRIPTION FOR CAUSAL MARKETING ANALYTICS

For marketers looking to conduct causal research, the environment has changed a great deal. Many of the changes affecting experiments are similar to those we've seen with other research designs and reinforce those conclusions. But their impact on processes in causal research is especially profound.

Initially, there is the ubiquity of data gathering present in day-to-day life that can be applied to experiments. In particular, a great deal of observation data is constantly being collected, so one can observe behavior, change an experimental variable, then observe behavior again, noting any changes. And all of that can happen without the subject (or competitors) even knowing an experiment is occurring. Given that much of the bias that can cast doubt on experimental results comes from changes in behavior when subjects realize they are being studied, this ability adds considerable credibility to experiments. In addition, causal research is sometimes avoided or done only on a limited basis because of the time, effort and expense required. With big data already flowing to firms and the ease of inserting experimental variables, suddenly experimentation is quick, easy and cheap. On-the-fly experimentation is possible and effective.

Independent, one-time experiments still remain of interest as well, as sometimes subjects do need to know they are in a test. Decision Insight's virtual shopper research or beta testing for games or software are not hidden in terms of being causal research though the actual variable(s) being manipulated might not be obvious. But the constant data collection occurring can still make it easier to conduct the research (users already playing connected games, for example, are already tracked) and attach it to a trove of background data. And the experience can be made engaging enough to take respondents' minds off the task, encouraging more objective responses. Further, the established connections can, as we saw in other chapters, allow communication research to supplement the observations. If researchers want more insight, reasons why the subjects did what they did, it's easy enough to ask. Such approaches can be quite common in beta testing.

Traditional test markets can also benefit from such ongoing data collection capabilities. In some cases, marketers will still want to try new products on-the-ground, in actual stores in limited geographic areas before launching nationwide. The circumstances are more realistic, they can run the rest of the marketing mix (e.g. advertising, local store promotions, distribution partnerships) as well, and can do so on a smaller scale before committing to all-out production of the new good. When doing so, retail partners will already have data-gathering capabilities in place at the cash register. Some may have loyalty or shopping apps as well, allowing tracking of in-store shopping behavior. Further, data can be used in context, so decision-makers are able to see not just whether the new product was bought but variables like day or time of day, what the rest of the shopping basket looked like, and pair it with data already gathered on purchasers, including background demographics and lifestyle information and previous purchase habits.

All of which goes back to the immense data collection, storage and processing capabilities we now possess. The number of subjects in experiments can be increased substantially without necessarily increasing costs or time-span. Dynamic pricing, advertising testing, Live Nation's ticket demand/pricing adjustments, beta testing, or any of the other examples we've talked about can be easily offered to a vast sample (or even entire population) of users very quickly and efficiently. Beyond that, however, experimenters no longer collect just a handful of variables as results. As just noted, when transactions, game play activity, facial or other responses to media content, or other results can be immediately tracked, associated data can be collected with them. Modern technology provides a much greater context for the results. Further, and also as just noted, identifiable subjects have histories. These can also be paired with the observable results of experiments. As a result, marketers have a significantly greater range of results to analyze, potentially optimizing many more variables related to their decisions.

Which brings us to one last aspect of big data and causal research that marketers should keep in mind. Deep existing databases and ongoing relationships with identifiable respondents mean that experiments can be done not only on ever smaller segments of consumers but even, potentially, on individuals themselves. We have alluded to this a bit already with the discussion about loyalty members and outreach efforts to get them back to a casino or resort property. There are also efforts by online retailers like Amazon to reach out to customers with personalized offers or communications. The potential is there to experiment with these at the person-to-person level, offering a 10 percent price reduction to Joe Consumer and only to Joe Consumer, seeing what the impact is on him alone. To some extent, Caesar's already does this with identified high-value members, and the ability exists for others to figure out best customers and experiment for ways to keep them happy and active with the brand. Big data tracking and marketing analysis of databases have opened up entire new vistas for testing customer relationships.

BIBLIOGRAPHY

Angwin, J. and D. Mattioli (2012), "Coming soon: Toilet paper priced like airline tickets", *The Wall Street Journal*, 5 September, online edition.
Decision Insight (2012), "Increase sales at the shelf", available at http://www.deci sioninsight.com/in-sight/7.12.2/7.12.2.html, accessed 30 September 2016.
Deswall, S. (2012), "How AMD used A/B testing to achieve 3600% increase in social sharing", *VWO Blog on Conversion Rate Optimization*, 12 July, available at https:// vwo.com/blog/amd-3600-social-sharing-increase/, accessed 15 October 2016.
Dwoskin, E. (2014), "Why you can't trust you're getting the best deal online", *The Wall Street Journal*, 23 October, online edition.
Hullett, K., N. Nagappan, E. Schuh and J. Hopson (2012), "Empirical analysis of user data in game software development", *Proceedings of the 2012 ACM-IEEE International Symposium on Empirical Software Engineering and Measurement (ESEM)*, IEEE, pp. 89–98.

LiveAnalytics (2013), *State of Play: Theatre UK*, London.

Nikas, J. (2015), "Now prices can change from minute to minute", *The Wall Street Journal*, 14 December, online edition.

Tarran, B. (2013), "Work in concert", *Impact Magazine*, **1**(3), 36–40.

Teradata (2014), "Procter & Gamble: Creating conversations in the cloud with 4.8 million consumers", available at http://www.teradata.com/Resources/Videos/Procter-and-Gamble-Creating-Conversations-in-the-Cloud-with-4-8-Billion-Consumers/, accessed 15 October 2016.

Teradata Magazine (2014), "Procter & Gamble: Journey of a lifetime", Quarter2, online edition.

Think with Google (2015), "Mobile video advertising: Making unskippable ads", June, available at https://www.thinkwithgoogle.com/articles/mobile-video-advertising-making-unskippable-ads.html, accessed 20 September 2016.

Urbanski, A. (2013), "At Caesar's, digital marketing is no crapshoot", *Digital Marketing News*, 1 February, online edition.

Valentino-Devries, J., J. Singer-Vine and A. Soltani (2012), "Websites vary prices, deals based on users' information", *The Wall Street Journal*, 24 December, online edition.

YouTube Insights Team (2015), "The first 5 seconds: Creating YouTube ads that break through in a skippable world", June, available at https://www.thinkwithgoogle.com/articles/creating-youtube-ads-that-break-through-in-a-skippable-world.html, accessed 20 September 2016.

5

Other topics in research and analytics

While research design and associated analytics are at the heart of this text, other common topics in marketing research also deserve some attention. Big data and marketing analytics affect just about every practice in marketing research, some more, some less, but differences are apparent. We'll cover some of those in this chapter.

DECISION PROBLEM/RESEARCH PROBLEM

A traditional marketing research text will often lay out the importance of establishing a research problem or research questions before beginning any information-gathering effort. This is usually predicated on some decision problem, some action that will be taken once the research is completed. A decision problem might be something like whether to change a price (posed to the decision-maker). Associated research problems are things the decision-maker would want to know first, such as what price competitors are charging, perceptions of brand value, and how customers and competitors might react to a price change (posed to the market researcher). Alternatively, the decision problem might be whether to run version A of an advertisement or version B. The obvious research problem would be which do consumers prefer, but more specific detail could include which has the largest impact on awareness, brand preference or purchase intent. So the research is planned so that it specifically collects data to inform the decision.

There are various reasons for this. Marketing research can be quite expensive, especially research programs that start with exploratory research to gain insights, proceed to descriptive research to add support to any hypotheses that develop, and then on to causal research to confirm the hypotheses. As a firm goes down the continuum, the research gets more and more expensive. Hence, "nice-to-know" research isn't often done,

Table 5.1   Useful terminology

Decision Problem	Decision to be made after research is completed (reason for doing the research)		
Research Problem	What research should be done or information collected to help make the decision?		
Consumer Bill of Rights	Right to know	Consumers should not be deceived about purpose of research or sponsor	
	Right to safety	Consumers should not have anonymity betrayed or be placed in any physical or mental danger	
	Right to choose to participate	Consumers should not be included in research without their knowledge	
	Right to be heard	Consumers should have an opportunity to withdraw before data are processed	
Sampling	Non-probability	Non-probability samples are not statistically reliable, tending to be used in small sample exploratory studies. These include convenience samples (selecting respondents who are close at hand), judgment samples (selecting respondents based on an informed opinion), and snowball samples (selecting respondents based on recommendations from previous respondents).	
	Simple random sampling	Statistically reliable probability sample, respondents are selected at random, all in sampling frame have some probability of being chosen	
	Stratified sampling	Statistically reliable probability sample, respondents are divided into strata similar within but different across (e.g. gender). Each type of strata must then be randomly sampled.	
	Cluster sampling	Statistically reliable probability sample, respondents are divided into clusters similar across but diverse within. Since each cluster looks like each other, clusters are randomly sampled.	
SWOT Analysis	Macro-environment (external environment)	Economic	Economic conditions (e.g. growth, inflation, interest rates) affecting industry/firm
		Demographic	Population statistics (e.g. age distribution, family size) affecting industry/firm
		Social/cultural	Social and cultural changes (e.g. religion, nationality, pop culture) affecting industry firm

Table 5.1   (continued)

		Political/legal	Political and legal changes (e.g. elections, laws passed, court decisions) affecting industry/firm
		Scientific/ technological	Scientific and technological changes (e.g. new inventions) affecting industry/firm
		Industry	Industry conditions (e.g. growth, concentration) affecting industry/firm
	Micro-environment (internal environment)	Company	Strengths and weaknesses of the firm
		Collaborators	Strengths and weaknesses of firm's network of collaborators
		Competitors	Strengths and weaknesses of firm's competitors
		Customers	Strengths and weaknesses of firm's relationship with customers
Competitive Intelligence	Publicly available information	Information gleaned from published sources, government sources (e.g. regulatory agencies), competitor's new releases or web postings, public appearances, etc.	
	Human intelligence	Information gained from knowledgeable individuals within company, at collaborators, or other acquaintances	
	Active gathering	Aggressive collection of information observation of competitor activities, industry events (trade shows), or more ethically questionable activities (dumpster diving)	

though that is beginning to change with some of the drops in costs we've been discussing.

Another reason is that researchers typically want to follow the scientific method. An unbiased search for the truth, as practiced especially in the natural sciences, usually includes a hypothesis as to what researchers expect to find based on previous research and observation. When doing quantitative research, this can lead to precisely stated hypotheses and alternative hypotheses, along with critical levels of some statistic that will lead the researcher to reject or fail to reject the hypothesis. The point is to reduce bias by setting the decision criteria in advance, so researchers or decision-makers who might prefer a certain outcome don't tilt toward that outcome because the statistics are "close enough". The precision also helps keep the research on target, looking most closely at the details providing an answer to the hypotheses.

In recent years there have been exceptions to these procedures, particularly as large firms began to invest in Decision Support Systems (DSS) and Marketing Information Systems (MIS), providing considerable data on a more regular basis. The growth of external partners providing periodic commercial research (e.g. Nielsen media ratings or retail sales levels) also contributed to this tendency to accumulate data constantly and without necessarily having an immediate purpose in mind.

And the trend in big data only accelerates the path seen in these exceptions. We noted in an earlier chapter how systems are set up to collect and monitor big data, whether transactions, customer activity, website or app usage, social media and other things. These are essentially the most modern variation on those DSS/MIS installations, showing what they have become. Decision-makers should be thinking about research problems in advance, identifying day-to-day data needs and creating key performance indicators to be tracked on dashboards. Much of the thinking is the same as in traditional project-oriented research, but established in a programmatic manner rather than on a more limited, ad hoc basis. Further, those specific projects can still be done, with appropriate data pulled from a data warehouse (or the entire data lake, as the expression goes) or being newly collected by tweaking the data stream. Using the example of LiveNation and UK theater prices described in the experimental research design chapter, the ticket seller had a decision to make on how to structure its ticket prices to maximize revenue or profit: the decision problem. The research problems included how theater-goers would react to different combinations of supply, demand and pricing, and experiments were set up to find these things out when they weren't already apparent. Data were collected specifically to address the research problems. So big data and marketing analytics can work to support traditional decision problem/research problem circumstances.

But potential new approaches exist that don't follow the established template and can be important in understanding the purpose and direction of research programs or projects. Consider the example of Amazon and other online retailers or service providers who were also described in the experimental research design chapter. The key point there was their constant experimentation, frequently varying website appearance and content, product features and prices. Sometimes this is just in an attempt to see how the entire market reacts to changes and sometimes it is specific to customer demographics, psychographics or behaviors. While each individual marketing change is in a way illustrative of a decision problem/ research problem, the entire range of experimentation is more indicative of a "try everything" approach – just throw it all against the wall and see what sticks. While the end result will be decisions optimizing the marketing mix surrounding offerings, the volume of questions asked is far beyond what used to be common practice in research. And unlikely to be supported by a structured, itemized set of research problems as presented in theory.

What has changed? Probably the most important is again related to the cost and speed dynamics of using big data for research purposes. As noted above, one reason market researchers have always been so deliberate in launching studies has been the cost. The potential downside of making mistakes could also be considerable. Test markets have always been popular because finding out that a new product launch might be a dud is much less damaging if determined in a single market area than after it has been launched nationwide. Researchers needed to take care to do it right, eliminating potential biases so as to ensure accurate results, because research tended to be expensive and unbiased findings were important.

The way research and analytics can be done with big data changes the game. Data are cheap and readily available. In many cases, when the data are already collected, there is no additional data collection and processing cost. Even the processing and analysis effort might be minimal. A retailer such as Amazon can change prices around the clock, and see the results in real time. Experimentation in this manner provides instant and clear results plus additional data if someone wants to look into it more deeply (e.g. descriptions of those reacting most to price changes, context or environmental variables). Further, research can be done as widely or as narrowly as desired. So prices can be changed nationwide, changed just for those using an Apple Mac to visit a website, or changed just for those visiting from Oklahoma City. Risk is minimal in many cases. Indeed, since nationwide changes can be done as easily as those in geographically isolated test markets, marketers can give a variable change a try, see what happens, and change back or in another direction if the results are disappointing. Research of any type can easily be repeated if there are problems or if the variable mix isn't just right. That takes a lot of pressure off getting the details exactly right for a single run.

Data mining and similar forms of analytics also show some new directions in terms of research strategies. Once again, there are aspects of traditional decision problem/research problem structure in some initiatives. The example of Target and the pregnancy predictor shows a clear decision problem: what can we do to reach pregnant women early (attracting them to Target for current and future purchases)? And clear research problems: what purchases are associated with early second trimester pregnancy?

On the other hand, sometimes data mining is done just to data mine. The idea of looking for unseen correlations or for clusters (segments) that have non-obvious but verifiable similarities doesn't always have a particular end-game in mind. One urban legend (no one can trace from where the original story came) has to do with a data miner randomly uncovering a connection between diapers and beer, on Saturday evenings, among young males (in their twenties). Sometimes attributed to Wal-Mart, the connection has never been confirmed. But the gist of the tale is the correlation discovered between the variables, which are seemingly random. No preconceived hypothesis was present, but a good story developed after the fact. Young, newly married fathers, used to going to the pub (the UK sometimes enters into the story rather than the US), stay in. But needing to do a diaper run, they will also pick up some beer on a Saturday night. The obvious marketing implication is to make an attachment between the two products (beer and diapers) and specific segment (young newlywed fathers) by means of merchandising, pricing, promotion and so on.

But the broader point is that sometimes marketing analytics, data mining in particular, is more about statistical techniques and digging into data than having a preconceived hypothesis or even a specific plan. This is particularly true for clustering, where sometimes analysts will identify segments with similar characteristics but have no clear path forward for what to do with them. They just know the cluster exists, has interesting commonalities, and there may be something interesting that can be done with it down the road. Similarly, any analytical procedure utilizing the updating of data, through machine learning or artificial intelligence, goes away from the "discovering the underlying, singular truth" approach of the scientific method. When conclusions can be changed given new data, the full truth is always still to be found.

In short, contemporary research and analytics is often based as much on rapid trial and error as on carefully thought-out decision and research problems. It's always good to have some strategy in the background, but the ease and low cost of frequent research initiatives have made them easier to employ quickly, perhaps as part of day-to-day data gathering. The research initiatives need to have a little thought behind them: testing out messaging strategies on social media, for example, needs some over-sight since digital outlets tend never to forget. But most initiatives can pass without anyone, even the research subjects, ever noticing.

ETHICS

The ability to conduct research on subjects without their knowing it, espe-cially experiments, should begin to raise some questions about the ethics of contemporary data gathering and analytics. And, indeed, the unob-trusiveness of many of the techniques we've described in this text, while very appealing from a data-gathering aspect, can be somewhat threatening when viewed from the subject's perspective. The huge amounts of data harvested from unknowing subjects every day by marketers and others can be deeply personal.

How does this square with what we know about ethics in marketing research? As with many things in this text, we operate with an established body of knowledge coming from the traditional manner in which market-ing research is taught. Most of such a discussion about marketing research ethics relates back to a Consumer Bill of Rights suggested in a 1962 speech by President Kennedy, including:

- right to be informed (right to know);
- right to safety;
- right to be heard;
- right to choose to participate.

The same general principles were then captured by the Belmont Report, rephrased as Respect for Persons, Beneficence, and Justice. The report has since become a standard for individuals dependent on US government funding and conducting human subjects research. Of particular note are requirements for informed consent and voluntariness as well as a reference to institutional review boards (IRB) now typical at colleges and universities.

But for-profit firms offering goods and services as well as marketing research agencies don't usually have IRBs to review research proposals. Neither do they always have connections to federal funding agencies. So what are appropriate voluntary ethical procedures?

Marketing research has always existed in its own world regarding ethics, as the practical aspects of good, unbiased research results can seem to be in direct opposition to ethical guidelines. Consider the right to be informed: subjects of research should not be deceived as to the sponsor or purpose of research. But if the sponsor or the true point of the research is known, it can bias the results. Knowing that Pepsi, for example, sponsored a taste test can lead respondents to favor Pepsi products, purposely or not. Consequently, market researchers will often keep the sponsor anonymous – not deceiving necessarily but not totally revealing either. Similarly, respondents may be clear that research is happening but the true purpose of questions may be disguised. Instead of asking brand preference straight out, for example, researchers might ask the first brand that comes to mind in a given category. This is exactly what projective research, discussed in the exploratory research design chapter is about: obtaining true responses by obscuring the true purpose of the question.

Similarly, ethical guidelines call for subjects to be able to choose to participate in research. In a way, this is violated all the time in observation studies such as tracking shopper paths through stores or even just observing their transactions, web patterns or social media comments. Researchers justify this by suggesting that consumers are fair game if out in public in a place without an expectation of privacy. Locations with that expectation (at home, in a changing room) are another matter, but anyone in public is fair game. Again, the reasoning is that subjects aware of being observed will act differently, so conducting the research without their knowledge or permission is the only way to obtain accurate data on behaviors.

Another way researchers justify hiding the research process or the true purpose of the research is to debrief. Nothing in the ethical guidelines specifies *when* a respondent might be made aware, convinced to participate, or be heard about any concerns. A debriefing after the fact would not bias results beforehand but would bring the subject into the discussion, potentially revealing all details such as sponsor and true purpose of the research. In any event, the point is that market researchers have always walked a fine line between conducting good, unbiased research while also attempting to adhere to ethical guidelines.

Big data has opened up new possibilities for research but at the same time poses new ethical issues. As noted earlier in the text, data are collected on a regular basis, including transactions, all customer contacts, social media posts, and elsewhere. Such data are often combined with other, external data, providing a full, deeply personal description of individual customers. Much of this is done without the individual's knowledge, though terms of service when establishing an identity with a website, service or loyalty program will typically note that usage grants permission to accumulate data. Once such data are collected, as also described in earlier chapters, marketers can provide customized marketing communications and offers or even experiment on identifiable individuals.

As might be inferred, these behaviors walk a fine line in terms of the consumer rights listed above. While individuals may or may not realize they are subject to data gathering, they certainly don't choose to participate in any specific additional data-gathering initiative. A right to be heard, including after the fact through debriefing is also generally missing. The counter-argument is that customers are aware of the overall circumstances – that tracking and data collection take place whenever they are online or on a mobile device, whenever they shop on the ground and use credit cards or loyalty programs, and just anywhere in their life when they are out in public, virtually or otherwise. Customers know and accept this because if providers know them better they can deliver better, even customized services. If they trust the intent of the organization, many individuals really don't have a problem with these circumstances.

A celebrated episode involving Facebook illustrates a number of the issues facing firms with big data capabilities and their perceived ethical responsibilities. In 2014, Facebook revealed details on a 2012 experiment it conducted regarding the impact of newsfeeds on user emotions. The Facebook Data Services Team routinely delves more deeply into the database cataloguing users' activities on the social media platform. Better understanding users helps to sell advertising and may be the key to new services that can further monetize its database.

The 2012 experiment was partially designed to answer questions about whether some users of Facebook felt bad when viewing all the interesting things their connections were doing in their lives (and then posting about). Researchers specifically sought to test how changing the positive or negative content of individual newsfeeds could alter users' emotional states. An algorithm eliminated designated "happy" and/or "sad" words from 700 000 newsfeeds, then measured the nature of users' own postings (by identifying similar key words). Although the results didn't show anything of real interest to decision-makers, when the experiment was revealed it generated considerable chatter across media platforms. At about the same time, the site OkCupid was shown to have experimented with potential matches between users, intentionally feeding likely poor matches to an experimental group.

Different aspects of the experimentation generated different reactions. OkCupid was aggressively defensive, with the CEO declaring "[g]uess what everybody: if you use the Internet, you're the subject of hundreds of experiments at any given time, on every site." Facebook was more apologetic, trying to explain the experiment more carefully so as to make it seem less intrusive. Although there were commentators upset by the experimentation no matter what, most users of offerings by these firms understand that data collection takes place, variables are manipulated, and, usually, the purpose is to improve the service. Sometimes this is for all users, sometimes for the individual, but better data leads to better products.

The new spins came from a couple of unusual aspects. Initially, it wasn't at all clear that the variables manipulated were intended for the benefit of the user. Just because there is a scientific interest in the impact of changes doesn't make them viable in the real world. It's hard to see how purposely making bad matches on OkCupid or manipulating a newsfeed on Facebook (other than according to the user's established interests) would benefit the user. If customers begin to question the intentions of these providers collecting so much data, the implicit deal to provide the information willingly begins to break down.

But the bigger issue, especially for researchers, goes back to consumer rights. The one we haven't really mentioned yet is the Right to Safety. Almost universally, organizations understand the need to protect the physical well-being of customers and so design and sell safe products. Most also want to guard the psychological safety of customers and so similarly guard against any such negative outcomes. But that can be an issue in marketing research.

Some of you may have studied the infamous Milgram "Obedience" experiments in the early 1960s. Stanley Milgram, a social psychologist, designed an experiment to test the willingness of subjects to follow the direction of an authority figure, even when the directions were potentially dangerous for other subjects. Obedience was based on a teacher–learner structure. The teacher was the actual subject of the experiment and the learner was one of the researchers in a disguised role. The teacher was placed in a room with an impressive-looking machine with switches ascending a scale noting shock levels from low to XXX, extremely dangerous. The learner, in another room, was asked questions. With wrong replies, the teacher was instructed to flip a switch and shock the learner. These shocks went up the scale as incorrect responses added up. Everything was actually fake. The learner was in on the illusion, including telling the teacher beforehand about heart trouble. The incorrect responses were made on purpose, and there were no actual shocks. But by the end, the learner was screaming as if in intense pain. An authority figure prompted the teacher to continue if he hesitated.

The Milgram experiments were criticized at the time and remain notorious to this day because of the impact on the subjects, the teachers. We'd all like to think we'd object if placed in that situation, refusing to hurt another human being just because an authority figure told us to. In fact, the majority of respondents did not object, going all the way to the end of the shock scale. Some did try to object but continued due to verbal prodding. After the fact, it became obvious that the subjects/teachers felt considerable stress during the experiment because of the conflicting emotions. Further, a number had issues after the fact, including after a debriefing. The experiments revealed them capable of behavior that they (and all of us) would have hoped they were better than. That's a very difficult truth for some to handle.

As a result, the Milgram experiments have always been held up as an example of how experiments or other data-gathering can lead to psychological harm. On a level relatable to marketing research, someone who is intensely brand-loyal but who picks another brand during a blind taste test might feel some discomfort after the fact – minor compared to the Obedience experiments, but the same principle. More to the point, the Facebook and OkCupid experiments seem to have the potential to deliver psychological harm by delivering consistent bad news to someone already depressed or by directly arranging a series of disappointing dates.

Some governments have already placed restrictions on data collection that may impinge on personal privacy (the EU, for example), and, in the wake of publicity from episodes like these, individual firms are also looking to police themselves better. Facebook now has a five-person review board, with both legal and ethical expertise, to look into research plans that may raise concerns. Microsoft has a similar review board, and the firm also sometimes asks external Institutional Review Boards, ubiquitous at universities, to review research plans. Big data and what you do with it can pose messy ethical questions. Users of big data, particularly marketing organizations who deal with potentially vulnerable consumers, are looking to get a handle on it. Setting their own industry or individual firm guidelines may allow analysts to determine their own fate regarding ethics before governments step in to decide it for them.

SAMPLING AND ADMINISTRATION

A couple of other key questions for gathering marketing data have to do with choosing subjects and then determining how to connect with them. We refer to these decisions as sampling and method of administration, and each is covered in some detail in a traditional marketing research course. We'll talk about some of the typical topics covered and then once again delve into what is different about new practices.

The initial decision in drawing a sample is identifying the population from which it comes. So a researcher should describe the nature of potential respondents (female, 30–39, mid-income, suburban, etc.). The research design will impact the type of sampling to be done, broadly defined as non-probability or probability. The former are typically smaller samples and go along with exploratory research designs which don't usually look for statistically reliable results. The latter are associated with larger samples aligned with descriptive and causal research designs which typically do require statistical significance. Non-probability techniques are often based on expert opinion (judgment samples, snowball samples), such as a knowledgeable participant or recommendations of the subjects themselves, as well as on efficiency (convenience samples). Probability techniques are based on random sampling, systems where all population members have some probability of being selected, including some more sophisticated versions such as stratified sampling (often for identifiable sub-segments) or cluster sampling (often for geographical efficiency). Nielsen, for example, uses a sophisticated blend of these techniques in setting its geographically, ethnically representative sample for television ratings.

If the population is properly identified and the sampling done well, the minimum sample size for statistical reliability in probability samples can easily be calculated. As research can be an expensive proposition, organizations will often be interested in an efficient sample, providing reliable results, with an appropriate level of confidence but no more subjects than necessary. Non-probability samples, usually much smaller but also considerably more expensive on a person-by-person basis, would typically also gather the results needed but not much more.

If we go through the steps in sample identification, recruitment and data collection, many mentioned in earlier chapters, we see some dramatic changes have occurred affecting the traditional thinking regarding sample construction. Initially, even if starting with blindly recruiting unknown subjects for marketing research, current technology enables an easier path by promising questions more attuned to individual interests and instruments considerably more appealing to prospective respondents. More interesting research more easily draws willing subjects.

But the real key comes from established relationships with potential respondents. On the observation side of research, subjects can be identified and monitored without their even realizing such selection occurs. As just discussed, this has considerable ethical questions, but if potential subjects are agreeable to being monitored by retailers, websites or other researchers, activating a program to select and observe the activities of individuals is simple. Quantitative data are readily available and qualitative feedback may be possible, especially if subjects are alerted to their participation in a study, enabling closer observation and the possibility of probing communication as well.

On the communication side, identification and selection of potential research respondents can be considerably eased if a relationship already exists. So registered website users, loyalty program members, social media or customer comment contacts, or other such identifiable individuals are naturals for marketing research and already have some contact information (and a willingness to be involved) on file. From that point, it's just a matter of convincing them to allow themselves to be tracked or to answer questions, and that can be handled with incentives or just an appeal to help a brand in which they have an interest.

Initial identification, selection and agreement to participate can be easier, but another aspect of sampling influenced by current technology is the ability to keep a group together, observing more behavior or asking more questions at a later time. Repeated measures over time, longitudinal studies, allow tracking to see if critical values might change. Common marketing metrics such as brand awareness, preference, purchase intention, purchase behavior and so on are naturals to be incorporated into a periodic reporting system. Such tracking can be done by recruiting new samples each time, but is much easier and less expensive (and probably more accurate) if it goes back to the same pool. Because of existing relationships and, especially, the depth of some of them, organizations can easily form their own ongoing panels or, as detailed in an earlier chapter, providers such as Vision Critical exist that can put together a panel for a client.

One other aspect of easy identification and recruitment of potential subjects is less focus on samples and sample size, especially when the research can be conducted unobtrusively. As we discussed in earlier chapters, descriptive and behavioral data can be gathered routinely from customer or potential customer pools. Experiments are commonly done by firms with an online presence, all forms of retailers and service providers, and others. When done in the real world in real circumstances, such efforts might not even involve a sample; they may target an entire population of customers, loyalty members, or more. If Amazon makes a price change or offers an untargeted promotion, for example, that initiative is available to anyone visiting the site. In such cases, the number of available subjects is so vast that sample size ceases to be a major concern. The initiative has been tested on the full population, so statistical reliability in extending the results to the full population just doesn't matter.

There are potential downsides to these trends. Loss of anonymity can be a problem when subjects are readily identifiable, though a lot of modern technology users don't seem to mind giving up personal details, including behaviors and opinions, as long as they trust the organization or see some benefit from it. Probably more importantly, long-term relationships and/ or choosing subjects from customer files do pose some other, unique challenges. Initially, researchers need to make sure these are the populations of interest. If gathering data from existing customers or from loyalty program members, those are the only views or behaviors you'll end up with. If non-customers or non-loyalty members are systematically excluded from the research, clear biases will be present in the data. Further, there is a real danger of members on established panels becoming "fans" of the brand, if they aren't already. Fans may not be entirely objective in evaluating new product ideas, advertising campaigns, or other ideas they might be asked to review. "Please the interviewer" bias can be present at a considerably higher level than is the case with survey administrators whom the subject just met. And, of course, these possibilities are present throughout the full range of research programs, communication or observation, qualitative or quantitative. Care needs to be taken with any results coming from potentially biased subjects.

Method of administration is also changing in the face of new technology. Several trends were already in place before the advances of the last decade, but matters have accelerated markedly in recent years. Method of administration, as discussed in an earlier chapter, refers to how researchers connect with subjects, specifically in communication studies. In traditional marketing research courses, the choices covered include mail, phone, person-to-person (face-to-face interviews, mall intercepts), internet and mobile. A lot of factors go into the choice, including response rate, speed, cost, geographic spread or selectivity, representativeness of respondents, complexity of the instrument, need for demonstration, probing, observing non-verbals, and others. A standard text would take you through the pluses and minuses of each of these, but the bottom line is that internet and mobile do almost everything better than the more traditional methods, especially mail and (land-line) phone. Internet is more attractive for many participants (including an ability to use gamification and other related techniques to make instruments more interesting), yielding higher response rates. It is inexpensive and quick, with responses going right into a database for immediate review and analysis. Internet can gather data worldwide or just in a selected community. Complicated instruments with complex skip patterns (if "yes" go to Q#44, if "no" go to Q#23) can be programmed in, easing the burden on the respondent. Interviews or focus groups can even be done with probing and/or cameras to add some depth and non-verbal capabilities.

Really, the only drawbacks to internet administration are an ability to be 100 percent sure who is answering questions on the other end and an ability to demonstrate physical products (virtual products such as advertising or games/software can be done online). Personal interviews remain the method of administration most useful for such physical product trials (e.g. taste tests). Mobile has many of the same advantages as internet in terms of administration. In addition, it has "in the moment" capability, allowing researchers to reach and converse with subjects as they are participating in some activity of interest, particularly shopping. Mobile also has higher penetration rates around the globe. Approximately three times as many people have mobile connections as have internet. Consequently, internet administration has been growing but adoption of mobile is growing even more quickly.

These same technological trends impact collecting data by observation. We've discussed several of these in earlier chapters, but the main point is that collecting data by observing internet activity and/or by tracking physical activity by means of mobile devices also speeds up the process while dropping the cost substantially. In addition, the unobtrusiveness of the data collection also provides advantages in better ensuring that unbiased behavior is observed.

In short, changes in sampling and method of administration have gone hand-in-hand with the new techniques apparent in all kinds of research design. It's not just the processing of massive amounts of data and the analysis of the same but the related abilities to gather the data efficiently from a large number of subjects that feed into the big data phenomenon.

Before studying the data, we can collect it from much bigger samples or even entire populations. And we can do so in a manner the subjects find considerably more interesting or of which they aren't even aware, usually yielding better data as well. The ethics always come back into play with these circumstances, but if those issues are properly addressed, contemporary sampling and administration have also improved research and analysis capabilities.

SWOT ANALYSIS

Researchers don't only collect data on customers, potential or otherwise. Customers are often most important from a marketing standpoint as marketing is the only discipline in the firm interacting with them. However, marketing, especially at the strategic level, also looks at other areas for pertinent data. This section will cover a couple of those.

Initially, SWOT Analysis is a major part of strategic planning in organizations, including within the marketing function. Before marketers make key decisions, they need to understand the environment within which they operate, including the macro-environment facing all such firms (opportunities/threats) and each individual firm's micro-environment (strengths/weaknesses). Definitions sometimes vary about what belongs in each, but such differences don't matter much as long as all pertinent factors are analyzed.

The macro-environment typically includes aspects external to the firm and over which it has little control. Monitored information can include demographic statistics and trends, economic statistics and trends, political and legal developments, social and cultural trends, and scientific/technological advances. The micro-environment includes aspects of the firm itself as well as its particular view of the competitive environment, in other words, the company's strengths and weaknesses, in all aspects of the business as well as those of collaborators. These are always relative to the strengths and weaknesses of competitors and their networks of collaborators. Customers are sometimes thrown in as well, as a deep understanding of customers or a strong brand image can also be a strength. In short, the micro-environment encompasses the strengths and weaknesses of the firm in question, its partners and its customers vs. those of competitors, their partners and their customers.

While SWOT is often thought of as a periodic strategic planning tool, organizations also identify some pieces of the informational inputs to monitor on an ongoing basis. As is the case with other aspects of marketing research, there is considerably more data available as well as the data storage and processing capabilities. These can enable big data and marketing analytics related to the macro-environment and micro-environment. Indeed, the monitoring systems can be set up with key performance indicators so that a change in interest rates or number of Latinas in San Antonio alerts decision-makers. The data can flow from several sources. Government bodies at all levels provide regular data reports, particularly on economics and demographics. These can be fed right into the system. News media can be tracked for political, cultural and scientific news, as can social media. Internal data tracking firm performance can shed light on strengths and weaknesses, including some of the enterprise and supply chain systems discussed earlier in the text. External data can also come from commercial firms. In particular, some providers specialize by industry, selling deep data collected from industry participants (for example, IMS Health, one of the largest marketing research firms in the US, specializes in healthcare data).

And, of course, there are providers with new approaches to data collection and analysis. In particular, tracking services have developed with specializations, such as healthcare and IMS, that relieve individual firms of the responsibility of doing it all themselves, often at considerable expense. One rapidly growing service is in the area of social media. Most organizations keep track of their own accounts, and those can include both positive and negative posts by customers and others needing action. But social media is a big wide world, and customers and other interested parties post comments, visuals and all sorts of things all over the place. Monitoring and acting on that from a brand perspective is a big job, and building the system to do that job is an unnecessary expense as numerous providers already have services with the necessary capabilities.

Probably the best known is Radian6, part of Salesforce. Such social media monitoring services use web crawlers to track brand mentions across social networks, blogs and microblogs, photo and video posts, reviews, and any other chatter across digital media. Key words and phrases as well as indicators (positive words, negative words, images, etc.) of feeling are identified and tracked. The systems are able to learn, so if a new word is used for the brand or as an expression of emotion, that can be incorporated into further monitoring. Dashboards can be utilized to track brand mentions and image across all the platforms. Recommended responses can be programmed into the dashboards so action can be taken when trends move in the wrong direction. And positive things can come from social media tracking as well, as new customer groups (or even individual customers) can be identified. Some studies have indicated that dissatisfied customers who can be recovered may end up being unusually loyal.

Radian6 and similar services are typical of monitoring approaches to the macro-environment and micro-environment, the process of collecting and sharing big data. Note, as we've discussed, how a lot of the inputs are unstructured (text, images, video) and need to be collected not just as data points but as data points with context. Imagining the entire web and a big brand, this can be huge amounts of data to dig through and less, though still substantial, data related to specific brands and products to store and process. This is especially so since much is of the unstructured type (e.g. images) that take up so much storage space. It can be categorized and organized (by sentiment, source, "influence" of poster, etc.) to help decision-making. Further, as also noted, there are applications to actually analyze the data for deeper insights such as appropriate actions/responses, social media user tendencies and so on.

But there are even better examples of how big data collected in this manner can be analyzed more deeply, the marketing analytics beyond just collecting and sharing big data. Trends in the macro-environment and micro-environment, for example, can be hard to spot early, but enormous advantages can accrue to firms that first see them and act. Trendwatching does just what its name suggests, collecting inputs related to activities by businesses around the world, then analyzing to discern broader social, cultural, technological or other trends that may be interesting to a broader audience. Such findings are then distributed in free briefings or more in-depth analyses to paying clients.

Trendwatching employs professionals in offices all over the world. These are the experts poring over the business press, releases from specific companies, and all sorts of unstructured inputs from the web. The experts also receive suggestions from a looser network of over 3000 spotters in over 90 countries. When one of them spots a potential trend, it is shared with the rest of the network, looking for supporting examples across the networks. All in all, the main idea is that the germination of an insight about a trend can come from anywhere; the information gathering is extensive and fed into the network. When catalogued and stored, it becomes big data (potentially part of a trend identified later even if not used immediately).

As an example, one trend receiving some attention was something Trendwatching termed "brand sacrifice". Divided into three subtrends, brand sacrifice included examples of sacrifice for self, sacrifice for society and sacrifice for the planet. The move by CVS to stop selling tobacco products, for example, surrendered considerable revenues and profits. But the firm did what it thought was the right thing, sacrificing its own financial returns for the sake of healthier customer lifestyles. Similarly, Tesco pulled candy from the impulse purchase shelves right by the checkout, again looking to encourage customers to think twice before choosing the perceived less healthy option. Sacrifice for society included examples such as Intel eliminating sourcing of minerals from conflict zones and Guinness pulling out of the NYC St Patrick's Day parade, given a refusal by parade organizers to allow explicit LGBT participation in 2014. Sacrifice for the planet illustrations were firms such as Tesla opening up their patents to "good faith" competitors, or various retailers such as H&M and Forever 21 stopping angora sourcing from China. The pattern is the firm giving up something, in a business sense, for the greater good in one of the three areas.

Based on analysis of the examples, Trendwatching suggested companies conduct a sacrifice audit, considering areas where they could sacrifice a product being sold, sacrifice something it is doing (e.g. supply chain), sacrifice something it has (e.g. patents), or sacrifice attention (e.g. declining an event such as a parade). Further, the report pushes firms interested in this approach as an appeal to customers to ensure that true sacrifice really takes place. Communication positioning some activity as a sacrifice that truly isn't is likely to be a transparent failure in today's digital environment.

The point is that even areas often dependent on qualitative inputs, such as these aspects of SWOT analysis, can be better managed with a big data and marketing analytics approach. Trendwatching doesn't depend on huge quantitative databases, though it probably catalogues everything its experts and spotters notice. Even if noteworthy trends aren't initially identified, these catalogues can be further reviewed later and combined with newer findings. What Trendwatching does do is collect and process a considerable number of potential real world examples, typically qualitative, unstructured data. Others, such as Radian6 and other social media tracking providers, of course, use tremendous data-gathering and processing abilities to scrape the web, store and analyze postings. But the end result is a SWOT process that can be constantly monitored and adjusted, as much of a day-to-day management tool as a once every year or two strategic planning exercise.

COMPETITIVE INTELLIGENCE

Competitor or industry analysis can be considered a part of SWOT Analysis. But the field of competitive intelligence (CI) has also developed over the past few decades, providing inputs to SWOT planning but also guidance for other strategic, tactical and operational initiatives. The short version is that virtually any marketing action can be affected by what competitors are doing, so information or insight into their initiatives or future plans is helpful to decision-makers. The long version is that CI can provide competitive advantage by allowing those same decision-makers to understand competitors well enough to anticipate their moves, allowing countermoves that can beat them to the punch.

Competitive intelligence is the process of collecting, storing and analyzing data, information and knowledge concerning competitors. Traditionally, this has included collection from public documents (general press, government publications, competitor releases, etc.), human intelligence (individuals inside and outside the company with knowledge about competitors), and active gathering (observing competitor locations, trade shows, etc.). CI's cousin, economic espionage, is chiefly differentiated by being less ethical and perhaps even illegal. The end goal of each is often the same, though CI professionals eschew activities such as dumpster diving, misrepresentation, cyber intrusions, and so forth.

Once the CI network pulls in any available information concerning a competitor, it is usually up to analysts to try to make sense of it. This could be operational, trying to identify or anticipate marketing adjustments or process improvements. Analysts may also look for more tactical or strategic moves, and predicting a major action by a competitor (new product introduction, new promotional campaign, merger or acquisition) is considered a big win in the field as it allows appropriate responses in real time. A CI team, for example, may:

- observe a competitor has obtained new patents pertaining to battery technology;
- observe that the same competitor has filed a plan with the Environmental Protection Agency for a new building generating waste products related to lithium ion battery production;
- hear from a contact in a supplier that the competitor is ordering large quantities of a specific material used in lithium ion batteries;
- notice on LinkedIn that a number of new hires at the competitor have experience in batteries and at automobile companies.

With those hints in place, the team may move into a concerted effort to uncover everything it can concerning the competitor and a potential new move into battery-powered automobiles, perhaps with a new technology. CI also has specific tools it uses to process and make sense of its information inputs, including techniques such as scenario planning or war games. With these and related approaches, analysts can plan out potential responses and counter-responses to anticipated competitor actions. If individuals on the team know a specific competitor well enough, they should be able to get inside the head of its decision-makers, allowing educated guesses as to future competitor actions and responses.

What is the potential for big data and marketing analytics in a competitive intelligence function? In some ways, the details are still being worked out as a lot of the field looks on CI as more art than science: the key is finding that kernel or two of insight within piles of data. It's often more about digging into reports and documents than quantitative analysis. But there is considerable potential of which CI will undoubtedly take notice in the future.

The LinkedIn example provides a hint, as that is a clear use of a massive database, admittedly third party, to uncover interesting information on the competitor (this was, actually, how observers figured out that Apple was thinking about getting into the auto business). But the basic point is that virtually anything that you use to gather big data about what is going on with your own customers or on the web can probably be turned around to monitor competitors. Consider several examples from what we've been discussing.

Social media postings can be tracked constantly, particularly if an outside provider is employed, but they don't need to be only about your own brands. They can include competitor brands, and you can obtain the same information on sentiment, level of chatter, specific issues (good or bad, such as a common complaint), or even rumors about moves into new products or new businesses (which could come from loyalty members or targets of competitor experiments). As with this type of monitoring for your own brand, it's easy to dive into specific postings for more information once they have been identified. So particularly positive or negative sentiments can be found, then mined for additional detail and insight.

Similarly, your competitor's presence on the web can be monitored. If a retailer, changes in prices, products and features, page layouts (if they are doing A/B testing, for example), promotional offers and other matters can be spotted. We noted that some service providers are constantly experimenting on the web, but current data-gathering capabilities would allow all those changes to be observed and analyzed. If a CI team has questions about the impact of an experiment, it could make the same change itself and see what kind of results it gets (assuming the target subjects are reasonably similar).

We also discussed how close relationships between firms and their customers, particularly loyalty program members, enable all kinds of research, from exploratory through descriptive and causal. CI typically has ethical guidelines about misrepresentation but if an individual is a legitimate customer of a competitor, there is no reason that interactions and communications between the two cannot be monitored and recorded. In reality, this happens all the time in traditional CI as hotel executives stay in competitor hotels to scout the competition, airline executives fly other airlines, and so forth. Extending those relationships to the big data world and close connections between firms and their best customers isn't a big step and can still be ethical if properly done.

PALANTIR

Palantir is a company highly visible in some ways (advertising and publicity) but also somewhat low-profile in others. The latter probably comes from early connections, including funding, with the CIA and continued work in applications like counterterrorism and cybersecurity. The company may or may not have had a hand in tracking down Osama bin Laden (it won't confirm either way). Indeed, its work was almost exclusively with governments until the early years of this decade.

While Palantir specializes in proprietary methods to analyze huge amounts of data, it also regards human insight as important. Specific projects can include over a million gigabytes of collected data, but these can often result in "data obesity" in other hands. As Palantir co-founder Peter Thiel puts it, the firm seeks to turn "dumb data" into "smart data". Computer system algorithms and artificial intelligence can learn to handle 80 percent of what is needed to process and understand data but the last 20 percent needs human insight to find something valuable. You might relate this to what we've been talking about with data monitoring vs. actual data analysis.

Someone needs to look at the appropriately captured and organized data, making sense of it all.

As noted, Palantir started with governmental applications, specifically termed "situational analysis tools". The process combines disparate data sources, bringing in all kinds of structured and unstructured data, processing it so as to be able to analyze it all together, and then subjecting it to study, looking for connections and patterns. Some of their important outputs are visualizations of the data, presenting insights that might not have come about just from looking at the numerical representations (or that may be easier to then explain to decision-makers).

Quite a lot of the data come from monitoring human activity. When your tools have been developed from counterterrorism efforts (looking for suspicious human activity), global human trafficking (also looking for suspicious human activity), or fraud detection (again), you tend to develop expertise in observing behavior. This raises the specter of big brother and surveillance since the firm does still have close government ties. But representatives claim the firm is actually able to use less surveillance data because its systems determine which observations are key and which can be ignored. With "smart intrusion", Palantir should be able to reduce concerns about privacy and civil rights rather than inflate them.

In the private sector, Palantir will go into a new client's organization, embedding itself while working with the firm to flag potentially valuable data sources. It will also look to identify any problems with the data collection, storage and processing systems. Some of this may be publicly available data (e.g. social media), some may be commercial data (transaction reports, market baskets), and some may be internal (much of what we've discussed in this text). Through it, Palantir can help all the way from strategic planning down to tactical or operational decisions. Though its activities are sometimes opaque, specific recommendations noted in the press include helping Zurich to price insurance policies better, providing a system for Intuit to better spot identity thieves using its products (protecting legitimate customers), using First Data's credit card records to advise small businesses on decisions like new locations, and telling Hershey's that some of its products sell best when placed next to marshmallows.

The example of Palantir has several implications for the topics discussed in this chapter. Initially, the mix of diverse, massive amounts of incoming data combined with human intelligence is exactly the kind of thing one looks at for SWOT analysis. While performance indicators and tolerance levels paired with algorithms can designate responses to macro-environmental (e.g. demographic shifts, economic shifts) or micro-environmental (competitor actions) changes, it is human analysis that has established those items as critical and the levels to monitor. Humans also determine what to do about those changes. The computer–human interaction is important in any application with big data but the human intelligence piece is particularly important with less quantitative activities such as SWOT.

As alluded to in the discussion, Palantir also raises questions about ethics. Pervasive systems monitoring individual behavior sound spooky and, although the general public doesn't seem to mind when it's Google or Facebook, firms with government ties looking into things like financial records and suspicious locations can raise more questions. Palantir is proactive in dealing with the ethical issues. Initially, as already noted, the firm makes clear that its processes actually reduce the amount of relevant data monitored concerning research subjects. The firm also has established ethical procedures, including limiting the access of data to those who actually need it for their job. Clear divisions exist between those working on a project who need sensitive data and those who don't. Finally, Palantir is also aggressive in pursuing non-profit opportunities, using its capabilities to help funnel aid to Syrian refugees or to identify human trafficking activity.

Palantir also shows some elements of competitive intelligence activity, at least the counterintelligence portion of it. The types of analysis the firm uses can be applied to track suspicious activity, whether it be employees who might take sensitive information with them when they leave the firm or unauthorized individuals poking around computer systems, Palantir can spot the patterns that indicate something might be amiss. For every competitive intelligence operations playing offense, there needs to be one playing defense as well, keeping the other company's spooks out. Palantir's tools are ideal for counterintelligence work, even in marketing applications.

PRESCRIPTION FOR OTHER TOPICS IN MARKETING ANALYTICS

Big data and marketing analytics are intertwined with the entire research process in today's world. The impact is clearest on the research designs since those choices drive much else of what happens in a research program or project. But marketing professionals should understand some of the issues affecting other parts of research. This chapter covers some of those.

One important thing to keep in mind, highlighted in the previous section, is to keep big data the tool, not the driving force of any research. The human element needs to remain, guiding the process and making sense of aspects the computers cannot. Some aspects of analytics and consequent decision-making require the kind of complex, critical thinking that isn't unique to overwhelming amounts of big data. SWOT analysis is a good example of that. While big data can be helpful to the process, good SWOTs come from identifying the important indicators in the data and focusing on those. Algorithms can be established to help feed the data into a decision-making framework, but intelligence must still decide what data to track, what tolerance levels trigger the action embedded in the algorithm, and what those actions should be.

The situation is similar in competitive intelligence. Again, there is a considerable amount of data available just in publicly available systems, presuming your competitor's internal systems are off-limits (legally and/or ethically). Again, the analysts need to specify what might be available and in what form, what is to be collected, and how it will be stored and accessed. And while there may be trigger points in some carefully tracked indicators, someone needs to identify those data streams and critical levels. But competitive intelligence, in particular, really requires deeper human analysis more than just monitoring big data. Much of it may be qualitative and making sense of a range of diverse, seemingly disconnected inputs is what CI analysts do. As noted in the discussion, CI techniques tend to be war games and other exercises involving not just data but empathetic thinking, including action and response patterns repeated across numerous time periods.

Similarly, we still have decision problems and research problems. These may not be as explicit in every case as what is traditionally recommended, but they still exist. The difference comes from big data systems that may be set up to capture any and all data generated within the firm, by collaborators, from pertinent commercial data suppliers, or from public sources. Even so, the human intelligence aspect again comes into identifying data sources. Someone has to see the potential in the massive data collection even if there is no immediate purpose. Further, in applying the data at some point, there needs to be a decision identified as well as supporting research. The big data monitoring systems need human insight, especially concerning the key performance indicators and what other reports need to be on decision-makers' dashboards. Similarly, someone is making the call in what data mining or analysis projects need work. With the data lakes available to researchers, they could go in any number of directions; the choice to look into Target's pregnant customers, for example, didn't come from the system but from marketers making strategic and tactical choices. Decision problems and research problems are much less explicit but are still around in some form. Big data and marketing analytics don't run themselves. Making the systems intelligent still requires the human input.

Finally, big data raises all sorts of new ethical issues. How you present the issues would be a good case study in how to bias question responses as consumer feelings can be variable. If you frame it as firms collecting details on customers so as to provide a better offering and potential rewards, many individuals find it compelling. And most users don't worry enough about the data gathering to bother with the lengthy terms of service agreements they click through when signing up for some of these firms. On the other hand, if you frame the actions as close surveillance of all customer activities online (and, often, in the real world), concerns are raised. In reality, of course, it's both. Market researchers have always had their own interpretations of what is ethical and what is not, balancing between customer rights and unbiased data. In today's world, when unobtrusive data collection on a massive scale is so easy, marketers need to take explicit steps to keep the ethical considerations in mind. Privacy of individuals should be respected and care taken not to do any personal harm. Legal restrictions on data collection already exist in some parts of the world and will spread rapidly if sensible ethical standards are not established and followed.

BIBLIOGRAPHY

Albergotti, R. (2014), "Furor erupts over Facebook's experiment on users", *The Wall Street Journal*, 30 June, online edition.
American Marketing Association (2016), *Statement of Ethics*, available at https://archive.ama.org/Archive/AboutAMA/Pages/Statement%20of%20Ethics.aspx, accessed 5 November 2016.
Chiang, O. (2011), "Super crunchers", *Forbes*, 23 February, online edition.
Finn, H. (2012), "New gumshoes go deep with data", *The Wall Street Journal*, 22 October, online edition.
Hernandez, D. and D. Seetharaman (2016), "Facebook offers details on how it handles research", *The Wall Street Journal*, 14 June, online edition.
Lev-Ram, M. (2016), "Palantir connects the dots with big data", *Fortune*, 9 March, online edition.
Marketing Research Association (2016), *MRA Code of Marketing Research*

Standards, available at http://www.marketingresearch.org/issues-policies/mra-code-marketing-research-standards, accessed 5 November 2016.

McNulty, E.J. (2015), "Can brands save the world?", *Strategy+Business*, 29 June, available at http://www.strategy-business.com/blog/Can-Brands-Save-the-World, accessed 5 November 2016.

Office of the Secretary, Ethical Principles and Guidelines for the Protection of Human Subjects of Research, The National Commission for the Protection of Human Subjects of Biomedical and Behavioral Research (1979), *The Belmont Report*, 18 April, available at http://www.hhs.gov/ohrp/regulations-and-policy/belmont-report/, accessed 5 November 2016.

Pulse (2015), "Ask the expert: Maxwell Luthy", (March/April), pp. 56–7.

Radian6 (2016), https://www.marketingcloud.com/au/products/social-media-marketing/radian6/, accessed 5 November 2016.

Simonite, T. (2014), "Software that augments human thinking", *MIT Technology Review*, 22 January, online edition.

Trendwatching (2014), "Brand sacrifice", *October 2014 Trend Briefing*, October, available at http://trendwatching.com/trends/brand-sacrifice/, accessed 5 November 2016.

Vickery, J. (2014), "Unknowing test subjects: The ethics of social media sites conducting experiments on users", *Social Convergence* (blog), 30 July, available at https://jrvickery.com/2014/07/30/unknowing-test-subjects-the-ethics-of-social-media-sites-conducting-experiments-on-users/, accessed 5 November 2016.

6

Analytics 1: big data

This text was written for students looking to be marketing professionals, more specifically those who will need to understand the role of big data and analytics in contemporary marketing. It's not intended for data scientists nor is it going to turn marketers into data scientists. But for anyone who needs to understand how big data is done and what the results mean, it's an appropriate primer. What follows in this and the next chapter is an introduction to concepts behind big data processing and some of the tools used to accomplish it. So if you need to commission a data collection and analysis program, you have a better idea of what you are asking for, what is actually being done behind the scenes, and what kind of results you will see when all is done.

MEASUREMENT SCALES

To begin, we need to talk a bit about measurement theory, something covered in traditional marketing research texts that is critical for understanding what analysis tool to apply and what outcomes to expect. Students often find the concepts difficult, but take comfort in the fact that contemporary statistical software will often determine the appropriate measurement steps for you. But it still helps to understand why. As you'll see, we'll refer back to these definitions in one way or another for virtually every analytic technique discussed.

Measurement can be complicated as we use numbers to represent items in different ways. A communicated "yes" or "no" or an observed "bought" or "did not buy" are usually represented with numbers when put into a spreadsheet. The relationships (yes = 1, no = 2) must be defined. Alternatively, annual spending on a product communicated or observed would be in numeric form when collected, so the dollar amount can go right into the spreadsheet. The dollar amount would probably include an

Table 6.1   Useful terminology

Measurement Scale	Nominal	Discrete measures. Numbers with no pre-assigned value, labels only.
	Ordinal	Discrete measures. Numbers must again be assigned but now the rank order has meaning.
	Interval	Continuous measures. Numbers are in order and distances between them are consistent. Zero is undefined or just another point on the scale.
	Ratio	Continuous measures. Order, consistent differences, and zero has meaning.
Cross-Tabulation (Contingency Tables)	Tabulation with two or more variables, cuts data into smaller cells by adding variables. Term is most commonly used with discrete or categorical variables, though adaptations for continuous variables are possible.	

explanation or description (e.g. annual, per household, US dollars) but the definition doesn't need to be as explicit. So some data results are quite straightforward, but in other circumstances we need to define what the relationships are, or they make no sense. Formally, numbers are assigned to represent quantities or attributes. Consider a number of definitions and examples.

- *Nominal* measures are numbers with no meaning beyond what is assigned in that circumstance. The researchers use numbers to identify observations or responses. The most obvious and perhaps most widely used example might be user/non-user (customer/non-customer) similar to examples we just discussed. In depicting that in a database (picture it in a spreadsheet), we might use "0" to indicate user and "1" to indicate non-user. Just as easily, "1" might be user and "2" non-user. It all depends on how the researcher defines it, and either way is correct. Once defined, we know that if we see "2" in a spreadsheet, it means the respondent is a non-user.

Nominal measures are a form of discrete or categorical data and are typically used with qualitative information. Metrics aren't always needed with qualitative responses or observations, so a spreadsheet wouldn't even be used. If we were tracking social media chatter or blog postings, for example, the input might be the text itself; it's stored and reviewed as needed but doesn't necessarily require quantitative metrics. If we do choose to try to measure such data, all we can really do is identify responses/observations that fall into a particular category, then count them up. If transferred into a database, these categories are then assigned numbers. Typical examples in marketing include gender, education level, occupation, nationality/ ethnicity, brand preference, sentiment, or anything else where there is no order to the possible responses/observations. When processing text, images or unstructured data, this can be done by categorizing terms, aspects of images, or anything allowing distinctions to be made (e.g. brand visible in picture or not?).

This is precisely how word clouds are done. One can examine text (e.g. social media posts) for every mention of a company, its brands, or related references (e.g. Apple, iPhone, Mac). If positive, those might be assigned "1", negative a "2". From the same inputs, all mentions of Samsung, Galaxy, etc. might rate a "3" if positive or a "4" if negative. And so on and so forth. Such results can be counted up in the database and presented as frequencies or relative frequencies (percentages). Or they can be presented in a word cloud, with the highest frequency categories appearing as the largest words in the cloud. In this case, you might have two word clouds, one representing positive comments on all brands, the other negative comments.

Nominal measures are severely limited in what we can do with them from a mathematical point of view. Counting is fine. The total number of responses/observations in a category is the frequency, how frequently that type of item occurs. If compared, as a percentage, to all the responses/ observations, we refer to the results as relative frequency. Functions such as means or standard deviations are impossible. The proper form of average is the mode. Nominal measures can be extremely useful for "cutting" the data as we've previously discussed, but have to be used within their limitations.

- *Ordinal* measures are a step up in terms of capabilities. These are another form of discrete or categorical data. Numbers are again assigned but there is an order to them. The order can arbitrarily go in either direction, so the researcher needs to define that 1 is more or better than 2, which is more or better than 3, etc. (or vice versa). As a result, there is an order or ranking to the numbers. These type of metrics are also commonly used in marketing, whether related to brand preference (rank favorite brands), feature preferences, media preferences, or anything where we ask or observe what respondents like best or prefer. Packages of features can also be ranked as when conjoint analysis is done: a specific research approach using ranking exercises to determine preferences and tradeoffs in product features (e.g. would you prefer more options or a lower price?).

So ordinal measures add the element of rank to categorical responses/ observations but we still don't know the difference between the ranks, the intervals. The difference between preferred brand A and brand B may be substantial or it may be miniscule, we simply don't know. Similarly, the interval between A and B may be the same or totally different from that between C and D. Each respondent is different. In another example, asking them how often they participate in some activity (frequently, infrequently, rarely or never), we get no consistency between levels or between respondents, but there is clearly an order to the responses.

Once more, these sorts of data have limitations on what we can do with them mathematically. Means and standard deviations are again not proper. Rankings are the obvious preferred way to present results and can include ranges (top ten) or percentiles (top quarter, bottom half). Median is the appropriate average to use. In big data sets, these types of data are again very useful in cutting data, adding that element of rank to the resulting analysis.

- *Interval* measures add intervals to the mix. The range of responses or observations have defined differences between them. What that allows is not just discrete or whole values, but any value between whole numbers is also defined by extension, what we call continuous data. So a seven-point scale on whether you think a particular brand is environmentally responsible (7) to not responsible at all (1) has meaning, and if we picked a number like 5.2, we have some idea what that means as well, according to the defined scale. Note that we still must define what number goes with what response, but the relationships are intuitive enough that subjects understand them. A number of very common self-report scales used in marketing and other types of research fall into this group. We often use interval measures to get a sense of attitude, preference and other consumer behavior concepts related to feelings and assessed in communication studies such as surveys. We'll talk about some of these shortly. But the main point is that the actual numbers (or some readily apparent representation) are right in front of the respondent or apparent in the observation scheme, so there is no interpretation of them. They go right into the database, and their meaning is clear.

With intervals, most mathematical operations become possible. Now means can be calculated for averages, along with standard deviations. Descriptive parameters or statistics can be calculated to summarize the data, and, again, the results can take any value, which is the reason why we can refer to these results as continuous data. The one remaining limitation on the data is the lack of a true value for zero. Zero isn't anchored, it can take any value, so we still have some subjectivity in defining the results. The seven-point scale above, for example, could be 1–7 or 0–6, depending on how we define it (and, perhaps, present it to respondents). Or it could be a five-point or ten-point scale instead. We would still get similar results. The example that usually resonates with students is temperature scales. Both Fahrenheit and Celsius are interval measures, and we can calculate means, standard deviations and other statistics to analyze temperature data. But zero is random for both of them and differs between the scales. Zero Celsius is 32 Fahrenheit. Zero Fahrenheit is −18 Celsius. The issue with that is that ratio comparisons are not possible. We can't say that 80 degrees is twice as hot as 40 – that doesn't make sense with an undefined zero. Similarly, a 6 on a seven-point attitude scale doesn't mean the respondent likes something three times more than someone answering 2. The results wouldn't hold with a different numerical assignment along the same scale or if it were constructed as only a five-point scale.

Interval data can be used widely in big data and analytics. If in the form of self-report scales and whole numbers, it can easily be used to cut other data. If fully continuous (taking any value, not just whole numbers), interval data needs to have ranges defined in order to cut other data. But regardless of form, interval measures are a natural for being the metric cut by some other variable (e.g. brand attitude cut by gender). We'll look at this a bit more when we discuss cross-tabulation.

- *Ratio* measures take the last step and contribute a defined zero setting. The data have defined intervals, as in the previous case, and zero has meaning. Number of units sold, number of customers, number of hits on a website, time spent on a website are all examples of measures where zero has a clear, unambiguous meaning. As a result, we can perform pretty much any mathematical operation. Means, standard deviations and similar descriptive statistics can be calculated. But what is different is the ability to do ratios. Twice as many units sold is unambiguously twice as many units sold. The meaning is clear and not subject to interpretation. Three times as much time spent is also quite clear. Ratio data allow us to do any type of analysis. Much like interval variables, ratio measures can be used to cut other data (directly or, more often, by setting ranges such as 0–50 units, more than 50 and up to 100 units, and over 100 units) or they can be cut by other data. And, as we'll see with all these forms of data, they can be used for predictive analytics as well.

RESPONSE FORMATS

Since the nature of the measurement has an impact on what we can do with it, researchers want to think ahead about how the data are gathered and what the results will look like. In particular, in what format do subjects respond? The same considerations enter into observation studies, the format in which observations are recorded. A little thought before the fact can ensure the right data are being collected in the right format for any later analysis that might be done. If you want to calculate means, you'd better collect data that can be used to calculate means.

Running once again through a continuum from most unstructured to structured, we can see the differences most clearly. At one extreme is qualitative, unstructured data, which is hardest to codify into a spreadsheet format. When gathering the data, these responses are referred to as open-ended. For communication studies, the respondents would be allowed to answer as expansively as they desire and responses are taken down verbatim. The transcript becomes the data. For observation studies, this would include raw video or images as well as social media postings or written descriptions from an observer recording impressions. Digital observation (e.g. web browsing patterns) could be included but is usually in a more structured form and so wouldn't be considered open-ended. As discussed above, open-ended responses can be turned into nominal or ordinal measurements with content analysis, word clouds, or any process taking the original open-ended responses and assigning nominal values or otherwise categorizing them.

Closed-ended response patterns include only limited choices. These are usually designated dichotomous or multichotomous, depending on whether the "multiple choice" format has only two options or multiple ones. Most obviously related to survey results, you've all seen the types of questions on surveys with dichotomous responses set to:

a. user;
b. non-user.

You've also seen multichotomous response patterns with greater ranges, such as:

a. never used;
b. used once;
c. use occasionally;
d. use frequently.

Such responses can also pop up in observation studies, such as whether a respondent clicks on a website link or not and/or whether their eye focuses on area A of a web page, on area B or on area C. It's good to have such options available for observation results but these are rarer than those for communication. Much of the idea of closed-ended responses is to make the choices manageable for respondents. The same could be said for observers, but with much of observation today now collected by machine, simplicity isn't necessary. Regardless of source, closed-end responses can become nominal or ordinal measurements, depending on whether there is a ranking apparent.

In some circumstances, self-response scales can be employed that allow the resulting data to be treated as interval measures. Even though just categorical responses, the scales are well-known enough and well-understood enough by respondents to presume they can interpolate the intervals between the responses. If the intervals are consistent in their minds, the responses can be used as if interval data. If one is to make this assumption, it's usually a good idea to apply a familiar self-response scale. When respondents have seen it before and when it has been tested and validated over repeated uses, one can be more confident in treating the results as interval data.

Consequently, marketing research employs a number of self-report scales over and over again. It is useful to note the distinction between measurement scales and self-report scales: both use the same "scales" terminology but unfortunately have different meanings that you'll need to keep straight. Measurement scales are the nominal, ordinal, interval and ratio measures just discussed. Self-report scales are response options for subjects, generally multichotomous, but developed for specific circumstances and intended to be used repeatedly in such circumstances. Several of these are covered in any traditional marketing research text. We'll look at a couple, as examples.

The best-known self-report scale is the Likert scale. Likert is specifically designed to go beyond consumer feelings or sentiments and evaluate the intensity of those feelings. As such, it is structured as a series of statements with respondents expressing degree of agreement:

a. strongly agree;
b. somewhat agree;
c. neither agree nor disagree;
d. somewhat disagree;
e. strongly disagree.

Five-point Likert scales like this are common but variations could include seven-point scales or even-numbered scales with no neutral choice in the middle. The point is that the scales will reflect degree of agreement with the statements. Just about all respondents are familiar with Likert scales, even if they don't know the name, and one can assume they are consistent in how they perceive the intervals between the choices. Consequently, we can treat Likert results as interval data, calculating means and standard deviations or conducting other analyses. So, the Likert scale is for a specific purpose: intensity of feeling in respondents. This purpose is of great interest in marketing, as consumer feeling towards brands, products, features, etc. guides numerous decisions. As a result, it is widely used, validated by hundreds of thousands, perhaps millions of applications, and so can be analyzed as if interval data even if not technically in that format.

Another commonly used scale is the Semantic Differential scale. Unlike the Likert scale, with a common set of responses for different questions, the Semantic Differential includes a similar question for a number of different scale variations (though all in the same format). The purpose of Semantic Differential is to uncover brand or product perceptions and it is particularly useful in comparing those across different competitors, providing positioning insights. An example might come from a study of ridesharing apps. Respondents would be asked to rate Uber according to aspects such as:

Convenient .... Not convenient
Expensive .... Inexpensive
Quick response .... Slow response
Unfriendly drivers .... Friendly drivers
etc.

Respondents might then be asked to rate Lyft or other competitors on the same aspects. The scales themselves could provide numbers (1–10 is often used) to guide respondents in their responses, establishing recognizable intervals on a recognizable scale. Once again, as with the Likert scale, the responses can be treated as interval data. If you've ever seen perceptual maps (multidimensional scaling), snake diagrams or cobweb diagrams, those are common ways to visualize the results, aiding analysis. But means and standard deviations can also be computed, allowing these comparisons across the brands.

Again, the main point is that categorical responses can provide all sorts of measurement outcomes (nominal, ordinal and interval) and specific, validated scales exist if the researcher wants results that can be analyzed more rigorously. So when planning the data gathering, it's good practice to think ahead to what the results will look like, inserting the response patterns providing those desired results. This can include observations studies as well.

More typically, however, a lot of the observation studies we've covered in this text go beyond dichotomous or multichotomous responses, providing direct quantitative data. Numbers don't need to be assigned because they are generated naturally from the observation. Transaction records, time spent online or with an app, number of social media postings, or even physical responses to advertising (eye tracking, heart rate) are all ratio measures to which any of the analysis tools we've discussed can be applied. Communication studies can provide ways for subjects to respond with ratio data as well (dollars spent, units purchased, number of alternatives considered, etc.).

To summarize, measurement scales are different in how they can be processed and analyzed. The form of response or observation tracking determines the type of measurement represented by the resulting data. Researchers can take this into consideration so that data monitoring programs and/or specific data gathering projects yield the results desired. Big data and marketing analytics require an understanding of these concepts and some advance planning.

ANALYSIS: INITIAL STEPS

For this discussion, we're going to use SAS Visual Analytics. Your instructor can get you an account through www.teradatauniversitynetwork.com. It's a free demonstration program for educational purposes and illustrates a number of the more advanced analytics techniques that we've been discussing. It also emphasizes visual presentation of results, something very helpful when looking to communicate results to decision-makers. Your instructor may want you to use a different analytics program, including a different version of SAS, or even a more basic spreadsheet program, but if you understand any one of them, you can more easily move between all the different programs.

If you go to the Teradata University Network site, you can register for an account using a password supplied by your instructor. Under the "software" tab, choose SAS Visual Analytics. This will load the module, and you'll want to choose the Data Explorer option, for now. Once it loads, you want to start a new exploration by opening the data set "BANK_ DIRECT_MARKETING". What you'll see on the left are the variables from the database. Across the top are the analytics tools you can use to visualize and analyze the database. We'll cover some basic activities in this and the next chapter, for illustration, but there is considerable, detailed instructional material available.

One thing to notice is that the program automatically identifies the data by type. So there are "category" (discrete) variables such as education, job, marital and loan. These would be akin to nominal or ordinal measurements, as just discussed. There are also "measure" (continuous) variables such as age, balance and duration. These would be interval or ratio measurements. One can change these designations in the program, but that should be done carefully. The software, though not perfect, usually has a pretty good idea of the format of the data.

The category details must be assessed by frequency and relative frequency. In Visual Analytics, this is most easily done by dragging and dropping the variable into the visualization area. Using the "education" variable as an example, we can drop it into the visualization area and the program automatically creates a bar graph by category. This is illustrated in Figure 6.1. By hovering a pointer over the dot at the top of each bar, you can determine the frequency within each category. Or by changing the "properties" at the right side of the screen, you can determine the percentage (relative frequency) instead. In this case, we have:

- tertiary (3470, 32.80%);
- secondary (5204, 49.20%);
- primary (1440, 13.61%);
- unknown (464, 4.39%).

You'll notice the system does not try to calculate means for these data. Since it knows these are categorical data, it looks at the distribution of the results, the frequencies of each category.

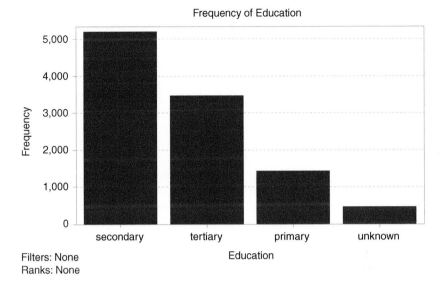

Figure 6.1   Tabulation example

With the measures or continuous data, on the other hand, means are possible. Just beside the name of the data file on the left is a symbol with two lines and a down arrow. Click on that for a drop-down menu, and you'll see "measure details" as one of the choices. Pick that, and a pop-up screen provides the descriptive statistics of all the continuous variables. Balance, the average account balance held by each individual in the data set, ranges between −$3058 and $81 204 with an average of $1548.53 and standard deviation of $3130.57. You can create a bar graph by dragging and dropping the variable – note that the program needs to convert the 10 000+ individual items with specific balances into categories to do this visualization. Otherwise, you'd end up with a very busy chart.

These results are at the very basic level. If you conducted research and were asked what the results were, these would be the first answers – essentially the results for each item on the instrument or each item observed. For categorical items, this would be frequency and relative frequency for each category. For continuous items, this would be the mean and standard deviation. Sometimes, that's all you need (e.g. gender, average age and average spending of our targeted sample). But, of course, we can do much more.

ANALYSIS: CROSS-TABULATION

The next likely step in a deeper analysis of a data set is to start cutting the data, as we discussed earlier. This is again fairly straightforward with the software. Good practice would recommend that you have some hypothesis in mind, some good idea why you choose one variable to cut another. But the process has become so easy that it's also now possible to take a blunt force approach and just start cutting everything by everything to see what emerges as interesting.

Cross-tabulation (also referred to as contingency tables) as practiced in this software requires at least one categorical variable. Most continuous variables can easily be converted to categorical (the account balance variable in the example above, for example, could be assigned to categories such as less than $0, $0 or above but less than $1000, $1000 or above but less than $2000 and $2000 or more), but for these examples we'll stick to variables in their given format. In a simple cross-tabulation of two variables, then, you can have two categorical variables or one categorical with one continuous variable.

Consider the first situation. Two categorical variables will both need counts in the analysis conducted, so back to frequency and relative frequency for what the analysis provides. As an example, if we drag and drop the variables "marital" and "housing" (house ownership) into the visualization area, we obtain the default bar graph. Across the top, we can instead choose a cross-tabulation visualization which creates a table. Note that you can change the appearance of your table, including which variables go on the horizontal and which on the vertical. Under the "properties" tab on the right, you can choose to add column and row totals, placing those before the rest of the reading or after. The frequencies in the table can also be changed to relative frequencies by creating a new variable. In the end, you can create something like Table 6.2 from the program.

In processing the results shown in the table, we can see that married couples constitute the majority of customers, with single about a third, and divorced a relatively small percentage. Home ownership is almost evenly divided, with a slight majority owning homes. Within the data, there are slightly deeper insights (single appear less likely to own their own home than married or divorced), which may or may not be a large enough difference to act upon from a marketing standpoint. Note that relative frequencies can be calculated differently (conditional probabilities, by column or by row) to shed more light on the results.

Table 6.2   Cross-tabulation example 1

	Single	Married	Divorced	**Total**
Yes (own home)	1511	2895	608	**5014**
	(14.3%)	(27.4%)	(5.75%)	**(47.4%)**
No (don't own)	1882	3047	635	**5564**
	(17.8%)	(28.8%)	(6.0%)	**(52.6%)**
Total	**3393**	**5942**	**1243**	**10578**
	(32.1%)	**(56.2%)**	**(11.7%)**	**(100%)**

But cross-tabulation can go further by adding more variables. The visualizations can get complex, but if you know how to use and arrange them, you can still make sense of them. If we drop in the additional variable of whether customers currently have a loan from the bank, we get a more complicated cross-tabulation. Again, with some rearrangement and adding in the percentiles, we get something like Table 6.3.

Once more, conditional probabilities could be used to get even more comparable comparisons across rows or columns, but even from this variation

Table 6.3   Cross-tabulation example 2

	Loan	Single	Married	Divorced	**Total**
Housing Yes	Yes	161	544	98	**803**
		(1.5%)	(5.1%)	(0.9%)	**(7.5%)**
	No	1350	2351	510	**4211**
		(12.8%)	(22.2%)	(4.8%)	**(39.8%)**
Subtotal		**1511**	**2895**	**608**	**5014**
		(14.3%)	**(27.4%)**	**(5.75%)**	**(47.4%)**
Housing No	Yes	180	296	89	**565**
		(1.7%)	(2.8%)	(0.8%)	**(5.3%)**
	No	1702	2751	546	**4999**
		(16.1%)	(26.0%)	(5.2%)	**(47.3%)**
Subtotal		**1882**	**3047**	**635**	**5564**
		(17.8%)	**(28.8%)**	**(6.0%)**	**(52.6%)**
Total		**3393**	**5942**	**1243**	**10578**
		(32.1%)	**(56.2%)**	**(11.7%)**	**(100.0%)**

on the table we can see some new things. In particular, married couples are more likely to have a loan with the bank if they own a home compared to other segments. An analyst could continue cutting the data in this way for even further insights.

These examples show how cross-tabulation is done with two or more categorical or discrete variables (nominal or ordinal measures) but no continuous variables. As shown, the results will be in terms of frequencies or counts within each category, and relative frequencies of the total or of any particular row, column or sub-row/sub-column can be added to help the analysis. One thing not shown here that can easily be added (with the full version of SAS or other statistical programs) is hypothesis tests. Usually, with this type of data, a chi-squared test can be added to the analysis within the program, determining whether the differences we see are significant or not. With big data we might not need to do so, either because of the size of samples (just about any difference comes out as significant) or because we are assessing the entire population, as is the case here with the full population of bank customers. But, if statistical significance or hypothesis tests are required, statistical programs can easily handle them (we'll see more of this in the next chapter).

If the cross-tabulation includes continuous variables (interval or ratio measures), it still needs at least one categorical variable in order to cut the continuous data. As noted, continuous variables can be converted to categories for this purpose, just establish ranges in which to put the individual items. But once you start constructing the cross-tabulations, the results will be means, not frequencies.

With the same data set we've been using, for example, we could create a cross-tabulation examining account balances (continuous, measure) versus job (discrete, categorical). Note that you will need to change "aggregation" for the balance variable from sum to average (that's down in the bottom left-hand corner). If we do that, the default bar graph shows us that the balance does, indeed, vary by job type and can be summarized by converting the visualization to a cross-tabulation table (see Table 6.4).

This is useful, as there are obvious differences in balance between occupations. Retired have the largest balances, followed by unknown, self-employed and management. Services, blue-collar, administrative and unemployed have the lowest balances. As before, we can add another variable to cut the data more precisely. In this case, add the housing

Table 6.4   Cross-tabulation example 3

Job	Balance ($)
Admin	1311
Blue-collar	1155
Domestic	1484
Entrepreneur	1800
Management	1882
Retired	2339
Self-employed	1945
Services	1018
Student	1467
Technician	1519
Unemployed	1363
Unknown	2120
Total	**1549**

Table 6.5   Cross-tabulation example 4

Job	Balance No House ($)	Balance House ($)	Total ($)
Admin	1611	1075	1311
Blue-collar	1547	975	1155
Domestic	1606	1195	1484
Entrepreneur	1707	1881	1800
Management	2003	1718	1882
Retired	2480	1569	2339
Self-employed	2346	1396	1945
Services	1060	990	1018
Student	1422	1727	1467
Technician	1663	1361	1519
Unemployed	1512	1029	1363
Unknown	2204	845	2120
Balance	**1797**	**1273**	**1549**

(categorical) variable. The resulting cross-tabulation provides further insights (see Table 6.5).

Throughout the table, just about all occupations show higher account balances for those without homes than those with. The shaded rows, however, show the opposite. In these cases, those with homes actually average higher balances. And there are differences in the degree of difference between home/no home account balances depending on occupation as well. The job of the researcher would be to look into this further, determining if this information makes any difference to marketing efforts and, perhaps, why the differences occur. What is it about entrepreneurs and students that generates different patterns for them in this database?

One other thing to note is that we have generally concentrated on using tables to present the cross-tabulation work. Data visualization software, including that packaged within statistical programs such as SAS Visual Analytics or even with desktop spreadsheet programs, offers multiple alternatives for presentation. Different people see the point in different ways, so variety in presentation can be useful in getting your point across. So it often makes sense to experiment with visualizations in order to determine what might be most effective. In this case, for example, compare the table with occupation vs. loan (especially without the shading) to a bar graph visual of the same data (Figure 6.2). The uniqueness of the entrepreneur and student segments is much clearer, as are the magnitude differences amongst the other occupations.

BIG DATA VISUALIZATIONS

The different presentations of big data and marketing analytics bring us back to another topic we discussed earlier, the systems for monitoring data. In the earlier discussion, we went through key performance indicators, dashboards, and how decision-makers use these constantly updated tools for operational actions. If web sales for a product drop off after a price change, for example, immediate action can be taken to correct the problem. Providing we are monitoring web sales.

The systems used to continuously collect such data, process it and present it as desired are quite complex. But, as with all these tools, you don't necessarily need to know the complicated information technology behind the systems, only what it can do. One can always hire someone who does know the technology. The key is understanding the capabilities, what you want for inputs, and what you want the end products to look like.

In this section, we're going to have a taste of what these systems can do. Again, we're going to use SAS Visual Analytics but instead of the Data Explorer module, you will need Report Designer. This really is almost

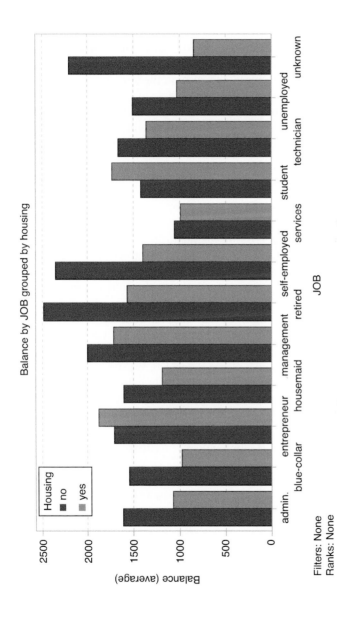

Figure 6.2   Cross-tabulation example 5

purely visualization software, no real data analysis is done. The user can, however, choose among a number of options for arranging and reporting the data. In the discussion in this section, we'll be using a different dataset, INSIGHT_TOY_DEMO. Within the Report Designer module, you can open up this dataset over on the left under the "Data" tab. With this module, you need to choose a visualization before dragging and dropping variables. Under the "Object" tab, also on the left, you can see the options, many of them similar to what was available in the Data Explorer module, everything from bar graphs to cross-tabulations. You also have a number of new display options, including maps and word clouds. Choose the "gauge" tool, which will be used to represent what these types of programs can do.

With gauge in place, variables can be dragged and dropped in. For a gauge, you need some kind of continuous variable, such as "sales rep rating". The dataset concerns a toy manufacturer and marketer, so we have variables concerning production, sales, customer satisfaction, and other items across facilities and continents. If you highlight sales rep rating, you will want to change "aggregation" (at the bottom left) from sum to average, as you did in the previous example. It's also helpful to take a look at the "measure details" from the drop-down menu designated with two horizontal lines and a down arrow (right under the file name on the left), again just as in the previous example. There you'll see that sales rep rating is measured on a scale running from 0 to 1.0 with an average of 0.37. This will be useful in setting up the gauge. Note that this is an interval or ratio variable – continuous in that it can take any value between 0 and 1.0. We don't know how zero was set, though this is likely to be an artificially constructed index, with zero defined specifically for the scale. In practice, this type of rating is probably some kind of accumulation of lead generation, sales per lead, sales volume, customer satisfaction and similar metrics. That would lead to a defined zero without real meaning, so ratio comparisons are probably inappropriate.

If you've dragged the variable into the visualization area, where you've set the gauge tool, you'll see the beginnings of your gauge (nothing will happen right away). Over on the right-hand side of the page, choose the "display rules" tab. This is where you construct the tolerances of your gauge, what readings would be considered good and what would be considered bad. This is also where knowing the range of possible readings as 0 to 1.0 comes into play; those should be the ends of the gauge.

Assume that decision-makers have determined that a sales rep with a rating of less than 0.25 efficiency is a problem that should be investigated. A rating of 0.25–0.50 is acceptable but bears monitoring (it should improve over time, not decline). Anything over 0.50 is good. You can set up your gauge to reflect this. Put in 0 to 0.25 for red, 0.25–0.50 for yellow, and above 0.50 for green. You should see your gauge pop up, with a black indicator line showing the average rating of 0.37 (in the yellow area). If this were an established dashboard, the gauge would update every time a new sales rep rating came into the system, keeping the decision-maker, probably the Sales Director, fully informed. This type of measure probably updates irregularly, perhaps every time the salesperson enters new information into Salesforce, makes a sale, or obtains a new customer satisfaction input. Other metrics, such as social media activity or online sales might be updated every second or even more frequently. The point is that the system can handle communicating such data and the gauges are the choice for presenting them to decision-makers.

And that's really all there is to it. Provided the system is set up to collect these data on a regular basis, the display or dashboard constructed to monitor them can be constructed as you see. We'll look at how to cut the data more precisely in a bit, but first take a look at some of the visual options for this tool. You can change colors, you can add more intervals. For the former, just click on the color option and choose something new from the drop-down menu. For the latter, just add an interval and fill in the appropriate new range(s).

The form of the gauge can also be changed. Instead of "display rules" on the right, choose the tab labeled "properties". The current format is "bullet" (and notice you could change that to vertical rather than horizontal). You also have the options of dial, slider, speedometer and thermometer (Figure 6.3). Try a few out. Further, you can vary the style. Move over to the "styles" tab. You should be able to see that the current "data skin" is basic, but you can change that to a number of interesting variations, including satin, onyx, charcoal and modern. The point is that you can actually make a pretty interesting dashboard, providing visualization of the data in whatever form you want. You should also now see why we call it a dashboard. With a variety of pure numbers, tables, gauges and so forth, a good designer can make an appealing and effective dashboard to provide updated metrics continuously.

One can also do some interesting things in terms of visualization and cutting the data. As noted earlier, tables are not always the best way to communicate cross-tabulations. The gauges and associated visuals covered here present similar opportunities to provide ever more precisely sliced data to decision-makers in real time. Instead of complicated tables or

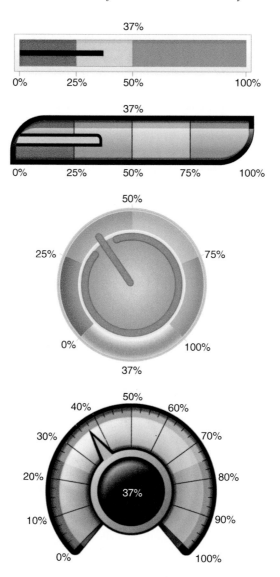

Figure 6.3   Gauge variations

streams of raw data, these types of programs can again cut and present the data in a more easily digestible form. As specific categories or individuals of interest are identified, these can be chosen for continued scrutiny and reporting.

Look at what happens when we add a categorical variable to our sales rep rating gauge. Choose the "cities" variable, then drag and drop that into your gauge visualization. It should automatically be added as a category variable (under "roles" tab on the right, slotted into "groups" under the tab). If not, you should move it there. What you'll see is all 32 cities (under "properties", also a tab on the right, you can select how many to display) and the sales rep rating in each. The gauges for the first ten are illustrated here (Figure 6.4). As you can see, the details behind the ratings are much more interesting than the overall average, with a wide variation in sales rep rating and, presumably, performance – everything from 29 percent in Australia to 95 percent in Colombia. As noted, a decision-maker would likely want to flag the lower-performing locations, setting up a dashboard to regularly report these metrics whenever they might be updated. The gauges are an easy way to process the information visually.

So that's a basic idea about how things work in terms of sharing and distributing data. Through that process, data might be categorized or rearranged, but, again, the deeper search for insights with analytics isn't necessarily done. We'll cover some aspects of those techniques in the next chapter. These systems are set up to collect, transfer and present data to decision-makers either as raw numbers, tabulated data, cross-tabulated data and/or in a visually intuitive form. Referring back to some of the examples from earlier in this text, consider what this looks like in the real world of marketing managers.

RELATING BACK

Where could we see applications of some of these techniques? We've talked about big data and monitoring systems throughout the book, but often more about the research concepts, than necessarily what is going on with the data processing behind the research. Reconsidering some of the examples and how they might be done with variants on the tools just covered should provide you with a better idea of how it all fits together.

Social Media

Consider first the social media cases we discussed. These included aggregation services like Radian6 and Trackur, research firms like Kantar that can plug into Chinese digital media providers, and could even include firms themselves. The latter can be done with tools like Hootsuite, allowing

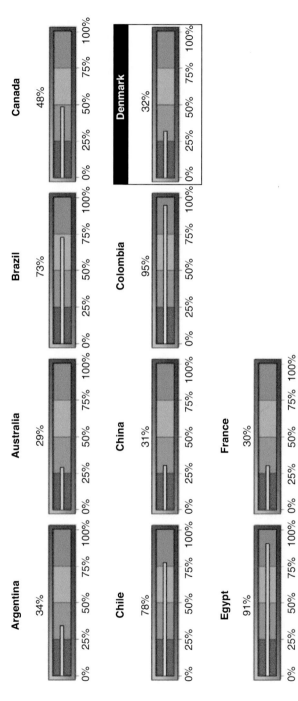

Figure 6.4 Gauges with added variable

an organization to create a dashboard tracking what happens on its own social media sites.

Firm-specific applications like Hootsuite or web-scraping tools such as Radian6 both operate in much the same manner. One should note that they tend to pick up both structured and unstructured data, though the latter is often of more interest. Structured might include number of posts, views, likes, retweets, and all those sorts of metrics that can be easily counted up. Unstructured would actually get into the content of the postings and the backgrounds of the posters. These are captured in full and stored (or at least their web address is stored for easy access to full postings) but then reported on an ongoing basis by the system.

In monitoring brand image, for example, a provider like Trackur accumulates all brand mentions and tags as well as any related sub-brands, product names, or associated terminology. These are captured and identified first by source. All the usual conversation-based social media (Facebook, Twitter, etc.) would be included, as would visual social media (YouTube, Instagram, etc.). So would news distributors (Reddit), reviews on retail sites such as Amazon, or independent bloggers. So the first cut of the data in reporting will often be by source/platform.

In addition, these providers have algorithms to classify items by sentiment. Trackur, for instance, includes good (green), neutral (yellow), bad (red) or really bad (skull and crossbones). This can also be done with key words, those that indicate positive or negative context around the brand mention or image. As noted earlier, the internet doesn't always recognize sarcasm very well, so changes in the indicators would invite a decision-maker to look more deeply into the actual comments, images or whatever. But the monitoring system is still able to create an alert that something has changed and someone should look into it.

Providers can also look at the nature of the individual posters. While personal data might not be available, their own activity on the contributing app or site can be harvested, including followers, activity level and other sorts of data. Consequently, each item can be assigned an influence score. A negative comment from someone with millions of followers is obviously very different from a negative comment from someone with only two.

More detail can be collected and analyzed, but these variables present a platform to discuss how such analysis fits with the cross-tabulation techniques just discussed. To begin, much of the data of interest is nominal or ordinal. Source is totally nominal. In the underlying database, Facebook, Twitter and the rest would have an assigned number as an identifier but the number would have little other meaning. Sentiment does have an order to it, so it would be more ordinal. Again, there is some numerical assignment of values to good, neutral and so forth in the database, and good is obviously better than bad. Influence is likely to be interval data. Providers would create their own metric to take the different inputs (number of followers, number of views, etc.) and rate them as an influence score, maybe some sort of 0–100 index. This has order to it, and differences between levels have meaning, as defined by the provider.

The data can be reported as overall scores, so a brand manager at any given company can see any of these indicators change second by second. Dashboards tracking key indicators could certainly be constructed. But the data can also be cross-tabulated. Different brands can be watched across the different indicators. Cuts could be made by sentiment, source, influence or other variables (geography, particular retailer, etc.). If negative comments or images of the brand are coming from an influential blogger on Tumblr, that could be a valuable piece of information. If the sentiment of comments suddenly changes on Twitter, that could also be important. If mentions of the product suddenly increase from influential reviewers on Amazon, that could also be of interest. The main point is that the data can be cross-tabulated by key variables, providing considerably more insight than just the tabulated results of each variable independently. Moreover, we've only covered the general level of these sorts of capabilities. There is no reason why a big database couldn't do similar work, breaking the data down by individual commentator, tracking anything they do, with any sentiment, on any source. So we've simplified things a bit, keeping the discussion to just a few key variables, but the capabilities of modern data analysis systems could take this theme as far as you might imagine.

Live Nation

Live Nation/Ticketmaster is another example of a firm where regular monitoring and cross-tabulation appear to be important parts of its data management strategy. As explained earlier, the firm is able to identify individual customers as it has an internet interface connected to its on-the-ground entertainment business. So customers log in, tying that visit to all previous data concerning them. This would include other interactions with Live Nation and could easily be paired with other demographic, lifestyle, or third-party data given credit card use and other identifiers.

This builds a profile for each individual. Live Nation also has data on each show at each venue and so is able to process which ticket buyers attend which shows (by artist) and at which locations. Further, as shown by the report on theater attendance in the UK, the firm is also able to add data on context of event attendance. That report, and others like it, include other data about nights out at the theater or concert, including total spending, what other spending occurred (dinner, transportation, hotel/motel, etc.). Note that the measurement types run the gamut of options from nominal (some demographic data such as gender) to ratio (dollar amounts) and everything in between.

From a marketing standpoint, this offers a rich trove of data from which to determine courses of action. Just in terms of monitoring data and reacting to it, ticket sales data for different events can be reported continuously. Further, if changes are made, the impact can be tracked in real time. So the example used in the previous chapter of Kid Rock experimenting with price reductions would be something that could be watched closely with rapid reactions (prices, promotional offers), as needed, if anything went in an unexpected direction. Similarly, the impact of ticket supply/demand on secondary markets could also prompt changes that could be monitored. Just from watching a couple of key variables, Live Nation and partners such as Kid Rock or a specific venue can react, judge impact, and react again as they look to optimize attendance and revenue.

The data can also be cut effectively for further marketing insights. Those metrics just mentioned, attendance and revenue, as well as other performance indicators such as attendance/capacity or total night-out spending can be cut by some of the other variables having to do with particular events/venues or marketing initiatives. These could be cut broadly by category such as type of act (theater, concert, music, comedy, etc.) or more precisely by specific performer. They could also be cut broadly by geographic location or more precisely by venue(s) at those specific locations.

So, for example, by various cuts, the Live Analytics team might find that live theater attendees in London tend also to reserve a hotel room and spend $100/person on a meal. Based on a link with credit card data, that group might also be identified as higher income, 35–50 years of age, and married. That could have implications for ticket prices, promotional partnerships, and some specific marketing communications. Similarly, discounted tickets might be found to resonate with frequent concert-goers in university towns, again with implications for multi-event purchase plans, pricing, event scheduling or, again, marketing communications. One doesn't know what the results might be but the point is to cut the data with more and more precise cross-tabulations in order to discern such interesting findings. The capabilities are there to even go down to the individual customer level, cutting data on background and behavior to the degree that the preferences and patterns of each person in the database could be understood and addressed. This might not be practical yet in terms of the expense of customized marketing, but it probably isn't far away. And there's no technical reason the data couldn't be cross-tabulated to that level of detail.

Bloomberg

Bloomberg has similarly deep data troves with numerous variables represented concerning its own properties and the individuals who use them. That level of detail is the reason advertisers are so interested in what Bloomberg media can deliver.

As covered in an earlier chapter, Bloomberg has numerous web properties allowing visitors to read news content, watch video features, monitor transactional and other data from terminals, access third party reports such as financial filings, and similar activities. In the course of its daily routines, the firm certainly monitors web data such as visits, content accessed (fully or partially, probably down to the microsecond), other on-site(s) browsing, and similar performance data for the business news and other offerings. Dashboards are both possible and probable, with adjustments likely to be made on a frequent basis according to these basic readings and to what an individual decision-maker might be interested in.

In addition, the firm would be able to gather additional data on web behavior of each visitor, registered user or not, through cookies and histories. For registered users it would have considerable background records, especially since many would have subscriptions paid for by their employers. So the data include not only individual information, including position and duties, but also organizational information that can be paired with the deep data already in Bloomberg's financial and news records. Additional data would come from any further interactions with Bloomberg properties including customer communications, social media postings and responses to onsite advertising.

From all of this data, Bloomberg can carry out the data manipulation leading to the products offered to advertisers. The anecdote in the earlier chapter about identifying oil industry or airline industry participants could be based on intelligent cutting of the data. For registered users, Bloomberg might already have the data on the industry within which they work. For unknown visitors to their web properties, Bloomberg would be able to use data on accessed content. If they view new stories in any form on the industry, if they track financials or trading results on industry firms, or if they do any searches related to those firms or on key industry topics, Bloomberg would have an idea that they may be involved. They can then use these industry distinctions to cut the data, finding other descriptors of those in the oil industry (other content accessed, background web activities, and perhaps identifying individual data or social media activities). These could be contrasted with the same data from other industries. Bloomberg could do much the same with cuts based instead on job title/level, geography, media preferences (video, audio, text), Bloomberg property preference (Businessweek website, Businessweek app, Bloomberg terminal, etc.), and so forth. Data can even be manipulated by how targets respond to specific communications once the advertising starts rolling out – their profiles can be updated with their reactions, including minutiae such as click-through rates, how long viewed, and where they went afterwards. And, as noted in other cases, the technology is there to cut the data by individual, especially if a registered user, if the firm wants to fully customize Bloomberg experiences and related advertising.

Beta Testing

As a final example, recall the discussion over beta testing, particularly of games. Remember that the growth of interest in doing so on a large scale came from the interconnectedness of the games, allowing huge amounts of gameplay data to be collected. All the details of players' decisions, actions, outcomes and so forth can be collected, along with key metrics such as time elements (when in the game, response times, etc.) and background data such as other games played (with similar data) and background demographics and lifestyle information. Once again, the measures could be nominal (some of the demographic data, discrete choices made at certain points during the game) to interval (anything to do with time). Data can be cut by any or all of these variables.

In particular, you might remember that one of the questions researchers were exploring was whether certain points in the game might be too difficult. The way to get to that would be to look at timepoints in the game, either down to the second/micro-second or grouped into time periods. At a certain level in the game, for example, when a particular challenge pops up, that entire span of time could be identified. In short, time could be cut by all the individual timepoints or it could be cut into longer time spans. Review that versus when "deaths" in the game occur, and you have your answer. With that level of data, researchers can zero in on any topic of interest concerning game play by cutting the appropriate variable in the desired way.

This chapter has introduced some of the basic capabilities of a contemporary data analytics software program. In particular, we've looked at analytic techniques for compiling overall results, the form of which depends on the nature of the measurement, whether discrete or continuous. Systems can be set up not only to collect the desired data but also to transfer it to decision-makers. Key performance indicators or other metrics can be monitored on a regular basis, and this software provides some examples of how the data can be visualized. Different data consumers have different preferences for how they want to see the results, whether in numeric form, in tables, in graphs, or in other visualizations such as gauges. The software also provides capabilities to cut the data more precisely, into smaller subgroups for more detailed analysis. These cross-tabulation methods are readily available in the software. Finally, the chapter has applied some of the data analysis tools back to some of the in-depth big data and marketing analytics case studies we've been looking at throughout the book.

7

Analytics 2: marketing analytics

Deeper analysis requires powerful programs to sift through the millions of items in big datasets, looking for differences or similarities between variables. As alluded to several times throughout this book, this is a different process than simply moving the data around or changing its form for presentation and clarity. It's more than just cutting the data, though that can be part of it. But as the analysis gets more sophisticated, the cutting is done in different ways. And it can be done with more of a sense of which variables to choose, as the programs can help with picking variables to test.

This chapter will cover some of these analysis techniques. As has been the case, we're looking at the conceptual basis of these tools so that you get a taste for what they do. With the software available through SAS Visual Analytics or elsewhere, you can get a feel for what the data scientists do. This won't prepare you for being a data scientist yourself, but you should be able to understand the basics of what they do and understand the power of the results and recommendations they provide.

PREDICTIVE ANALYTICS: LINEAR REGRESSION CONCEPTS

One of the most valuable capabilities of marketing analytics is using data to predict consumer response. Other applications of prediction can also be useful but much of what we see with big data relates to the trove concerning consumers, so we will focus on that in many of these applications. It certainly makes it easier to understand some of the concepts behind the analytical tools.

You may have studied linear regression in a previous statistics course. The basic idea is that you accumulate independent variables (x's) you think may be correlated with a dependent variable (y). Regression fits a line

Table 7.1   Useful terminology

Regression	Dependent variable (y)	Variable to be predicted by the regression equation
	Independent variable (x)	One or more variables used to predict the dependent variable
	Simple regression	Regression with only a single independent variable
	Multiple regression	Regression with two or more independent variables
	Logistic regression	Regression with a limited dependent variable (can only take on certain values, as when nominal)
	y-intercept (a)	Constant value in the regression equation
	Slope coefficient (b)	Coefficient(s) paired with all dependent variables in regression equation. Amount y changes given a one-unit change in indicated x.
	R^2	Quality measure of equation. Ratio of explained variation in y to total variation in y (i.e. percentage of variation explained by equation).
Decision Trees	Branch	Visually, when a variable is split between different values, branches form for each part of the split
	Leaf	Branch with no further splits, ends in a leaf
Cluster Analysis	Centroid	Mid-point of each cluster formed in the analysis. Randomly chosen to begin, moved and adjusted until total distance from all observations to assigned centroid is minimized.

to data points, the best-fitting line possible in terms of minimizing the error between the actual values of y and the predicted values of y, given its relationship with the independent variables. The math is complicated, especially as the number of independent variables increase, but the core concept of fitting a line to data is fairly simple. The key is understanding what data you are feeding the analytics software and then properly interpreting the results.

Consider Figure 7.1, employing some of the data from the toy company example used in the previous chapter (INSIGHT_TOY_DEMO). We have

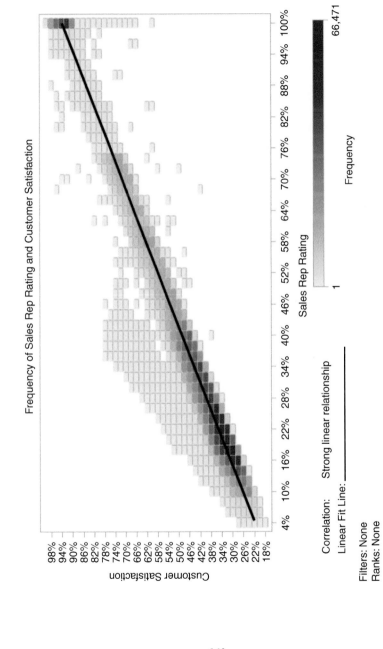

Figure 7.1   Regression visualization

data on sales rep rating, which is how customers assess the performance of their salesperson. One might expect that a sales rep that the customer likes would be helpful in maintaining customer satisfaction. If so, the independent variable (sales rep rating) is expected to be correlated with the dependent variable (customer satisfaction). Indeed, if we plot the values, we get the pattern seen in the figure (note that this is a heat map, accumulating observations – there are too many data points for a regular scatter plot of distinct values). As one variable increases in value, the other does as well. This implies a positive relationship, and one can fit an upward sloping line to the data, as shown. Completing a regression would provide the equation of the line and summary statistics of quality (goodness of fit). Note that you can replicate this figure by firing up the SAS Visual Analytics Data Explorer module with this database, dropping those two variables into the visualization, and choosing scatter plot or heat map.

Regression can handle any kind of data, continuous or discrete. For the independent variables, you just insert them – you don't have to worry about whether the inputs are nominal, ordinal, interval or ratio. Newer, more advanced forms of regression, referred to as mixed models, actually do handle the discrete variables differently (creating separate regression lines for each variable value). And you can see some of that in the output of this statistical program. But for our purposes, it's way beyond the level we're introducing here and not critical to understanding the results.

Whether the dependent variable is categorical or not does make a difference. Standard regression is set up to predict continuous variables, those that can take any value along a given range (and can go beyond the range in the case of trends). But if the dependent variable can only be certain values (e.g. 0 = non-customer; 1 = customer), then special techniques need to be used to make the prediction. Again, there is considerable and complex theory as well as complex math behind the specialized techniques, so we'll only touch upon those. But you do need to recognize the need to use what we call "logistical regression" when predicting a limited dependent variable.

Linear regression, as the name indicates, is about lines. If you have two variables, x and y, and have multiple paired observations, you can create a scatter plot of the values (note that here we use the term "observation" for each piece of data regardless of whether it comes from a communication or observation collection technique). Just picture a typical x/y graph with dots indicating the observations. The tool of linear regression simply fits a line to those data points, minimizing unexplained error between the actual y values and the predicted y values. The formula for this line is $y = a + bx$, where each observed x value could be inserted into the equation to generate the predicted y. And if a new x value came along, we could predict an associated y value, with some degree of confidence.

When we do analysis with a single independent variable, we refer to it as simple regression. Simple regression, with only two variables, can be visualized in two dimensions as in the scatter plot, so it's useful for understanding regression. But the technique can be used with many more independent variables. Multiple regression includes two or more independent (x) variables, determining their correlation with a single dependent (y) variable. All of the outputs are similar, though the linear equation is much more complicated and, of course, we can't visualize in multiple dimensions. There can also be concerns about how correlations between the independent variables themselves affect some of the metrics we use to understand regression output. But, for the most part, the inputs, process and outputs are similar.

One important thing to understand about regression is that any data entered will generate a result. You will always get an equation as output. That doesn't mean it's any good. So we need to evaluate regression results in order to determine their quality and how much we can rely on them. We assess regression results both in total and in looking at the individual components of the equation. Consider the standard results we look for in any regression output.

Initially, the equation of the line is obviously a key part of any output. This would include the y-intercept (a) and one or more slope coefficients (b) that form the $y = a + bx$ equation noted earlier. When multiple independent variables are included, the equation is simply extended:

$$y = a + b_1x_1 + b_2x_2 + \ldots + b_nx_n$$

The output will include the y-intercept and all slopes requested. The y-intercept or constant (a) is the point at which the equation intersects the y-axis if all the x's are zero. It can generally be interpreted as the constant, the value the dependent variable takes without the influence of the independent variables (though not always; sometimes it just makes the math work out). The slope coefficient (b) is the amount y will change for every unit change in x. If we had a regression equation of $y = 10 + 3x$, for example, y would be 10 when x is 0 but increases by 3 for every unit increase in x. So if x is 1, y will be 13. If x is 2, y will be 16. And so forth.

As noted, asking for a regression equation will yield a regression equation. One question to ask about such results is whether the components are all significant. Put differently, are all the components contributing to the explanatory or predictive power of the equation? Or are some more important than others? Statistical software will generate a t-test for each component, assessing whether its explanatory power is greater than just substituting zero for it (i.e. leaving it out altogether). A good rule of thumb for this process is to remember 2, since 95 percent confidence in a t-test is very close to 2 (1.96). If the t-test has a value above 2, the equation component is significant at the 95 percent confidence level. In this case, we would specifically be testing whether the slope coefficient, 3, is significantly different from 0. We would also test the constant, 10, and whether that is significantly different from 0. If both have t-values above 2, we know with 95 percent confidence that they are important to the equation.

Assessing components gets increasingly important as more potential variables are tried as part of the regression equation. If you had five independent variables (x's), for example, t-tests would be available for all of them. Some might be critically important to the equation. Others might not. For purposes relating to both the quality of the equation and, particularly, its explanatory power and logic, we typically want to include only those variables that are making a significant contribution. So part of investigating what form of a regression equation to use is the process of evaluating the individual variables. Those that are significant and important are kept. Those without significant contributions are dropped out.

The quality of the overall equation can also be assessed. There are several metrics for this, and they pretty much agree in their overall conclusion though they are measuring different things. The standard error of the estimate, for example, looks at the total error, the differences between what the equation would have predicted for y versus the observed value of y. Again, the technique gives us the line that minimizes such error, but this metric tells us the exact amount of that totaled error which can be assessed versus the magnitude of the prediction (an average error of 1 is very different if the magnitude of the variable is 1 than if that magnitude is 100000). Another option is the F-test for significance. This is a formal statistical test, essentially judging whether the equation does a better job of prediction than could be done by just guessing the average value of y each time. Most statistical programs give back an F-statistic that tells us whether there is a difference that is statistically significant given some level of confidence (95 percent, 99 percent, etc.).

But the most common statistic used to judge the overall quality of a regression equation is the R^2 metric. R^2 runs from 0 to 1 and is essentially a percentage of the explained variance in the dependent variable (y) to the total variance of that variable. So, how much of y's movements can we explain in a regression equation? The higher the value, the better, but what is a good number? It depends. Traditionally, R^2's in physical sciences, with a high degree of variable control, are very near 1.0, while in social sciences, with messy field research and low variable control, they can be closer to 0. In marketing or other business applications, we often look for the best predictor, whatever it is, but definitely something that grants confidence in the results (0.70 or more), at least when samples are involved. Once again, with big data and analysis of full populations, even lower readings may be interesting as there is no sampling error (e.g. a 0.05 increase in understanding the full population might be worthwhile in some applications). So it really depends, there is no hard and fast number for R^2 that is good or bad in all circumstances. But if you have options, you want the regression equation generating the highest one.

PREDICTIVE ANALYTICS: LINEAR REGRESSION EXAMPLES

To see these elements in action, let's go back to SAS Visual Analytics Data Explorer. If you already have the INSIGHT_TOY_DEMO data file loaded, you can continue with the Customer Satisfaction and Sales Rep Rating variables from the scatter plot/heat map example earlier. Or load them now. But instead of the heat map, we now want the "linear regression" visualization, the tile at the top showing a scatter plot and line drawn through it. When the visualization pops up, make sure that the "Roles" tab on the right shows Customer Satisfaction as the "Response" (y or the dependent variable). Sales Rep Rating should be in the "Continuous Effects" box (x or the independent variable). We're not going to use most of them, but look at the number and variety of additional options in this tab. Also take a look at the range of output visualizations and pay attention to the other output options we'll be looking at. Regression is a valuable, flexible and complex tool. Graduate degrees are available for studying regression. We're only scratching the surface. So understand that you'll have a little bit of knowledge about regression but there will remain a great deal still to be discovered.

In terms of results, you can see right on this initial visualization in Figure 7.2 that the $R^2 = 0.9736$ is based on 3.6 million observations. That's an excellent R^2 in just about any circumstances. The upper left-hand panel,

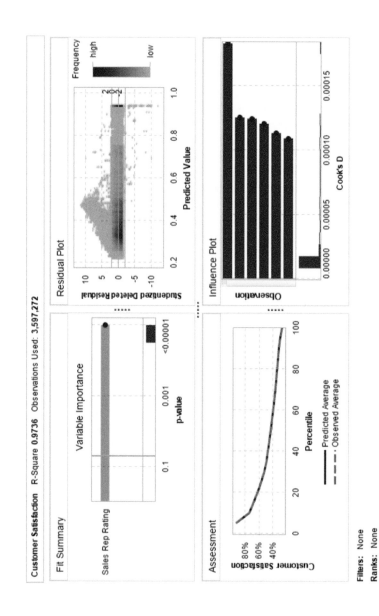

Figure 7.2   Regression example #1

"Fit Summary" shows the results of the t-test for the independent variable (Sales Rep Rating), which is significant at the 99.99 percent level (subtract the p-value from 1.0 to get the confidence or significance level).

The actual equation and summary statistics themselves can be revealed below. In the same line where you see the R^2 value, on the far right, you should be able to see a tile with rows of dots on it. Hover over it, and it will reveal "Show Details". Click on that, and you will see the details at the bottom of the visualization. Choose the "Parameter Estimates" tab. There, in the "Estimate" column, you'll see the results for the intercept (*a*) term, 0.1879 and for the slope coefficient (*b*), 0.7499. The t-value for each component is two columns down under "tValue", 6701 and 11 522, respectively. As shown by the significance levels, both of these are well above the rule of thumb of >2.0 for t-tests. Both parts of the equation are important, the intercept and the variable.

The overall indicators of quality are under the tab "Fit Statistics". Click on that, and you'll again see the R^2, the Mean Square Error (0.00075), and the F-test result (F Value for Model = 132 million, confidence level >99.99 percent given Pr>F = 0). As noted, the three summary measures tend to agree and all show an excellent fit provided by this equation. We could confidently conclude that a high sales rep rating is correlated with high customer satisfaction.

In summary, with a common notation for these kinds of results:

$$Y = 0.1879 + 0.7499\ X \qquad R^2 = 0.9736$$
$$(6701) \quad (11522) \qquad MSE = 0.00075$$
$$F = 132\,000\,000$$

For a more complex example, start a new exploration and load the data set ORGANICS_VISTAT. This is a database concerning organics purchases at groceries in the UK. What we want to do is build a profile of the type of customer more likely to buy organics, so we use "organics purchase", a categorical variable indicating whether or not the individual buys organics, as the dependent variable *y*. As noted earlier, when we do that, we have to use a special form of regression: logistical regression. Choose that visualization (dots in columns, the tile to the right of linear regression). Pull in the organics purchase variable, and the software should automatically assign it as the "Response" variable under the "Roles" tab at the right. In addition, drag and drop the variables Loyalty Card Tenure, Age, Affluence Grade,

Recent 12 Month Purchases, and Gender. Loyalty card tenure reflects how long consumers have been loyalty program members. Affluence grade is a constructed index representing affluence, probably the consumer's level of income. Recent 12 month purchases shows spending at the grocery over the previous year. All of these, along with age, are continuous variables. Gender is categorical.

Once again, the results are fairly easy to obtain. The default visualization (Figure 7.3) shows an R^2 of 0.2306, which is not great but it may be of use in this type of project – out of almost 1.5 million customers, identifying a quarter of the variables associated with organics purchase behavior could be helpful to marketers. And the Fit Summary for the individual variables shows that all are significant except recent 12 month purchases (upper left-hand corner).

Clicking on the "Show Details" dots in the upper right-hand area of the visualization again provides more detailed output. Once again, choose the "Parameter Estimates" tab. These show:

- Intercept   −2.096   −22.24 (z-value)
- Loyalty card   0.006   10.21
- Age   −0.534   −295.81
- Affluence   0.256   354.02
- Recent 12   −1.8 E-6   −0.08
- Gender F   1.80   225.39
- Gender M   0.85   95.64
- Gender U   0.0

As you might recall from statistics, the z-test and t-test are much the same thing, just used in different circumstances (usually to do with sample size). But the rule of 2 still applies, so all of the independent variables are significant except for recent purchases (the "Recent 12" variable with a z-value of −0.08). The parameters for the equation are shown. The negative signs do have meaning for the variables: they show the relationship between each independent variable and the dependent variable. So as loyalty card tenure and affluence go up, consumers are more likely to buy organic. As age goes up, consumers are less likely to buy organic. As briefly mentioned earlier, regression software can divide a categorical independent variable like gender and create different equations for each option. So this output shows three different equations: one including the observations with female respondents, one with male respondents, and one with unknown respondents (which drops the gender variable entirely). Female and male

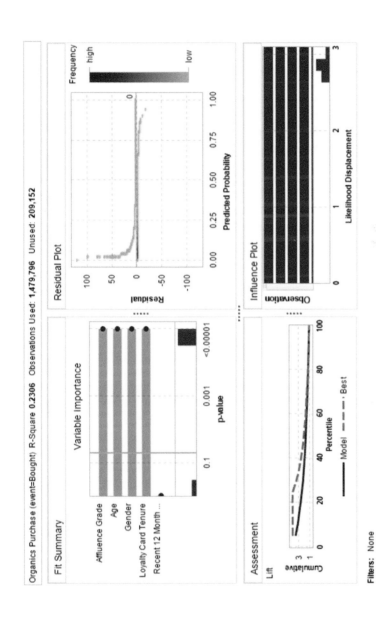

Figure 7.3   Regression example #2

171

are both positively associated with organics, though female has the larger impact.

For overall fit statistics, we have only the R^2 as standard error has little meaning for a categorical variable (the prediction is the expected outcome or it isn't) and the F-statistic also has some issues. As noted, it is relatively low but given the strength of the individual variables, these could be useful results for marketers anyway. In a grocery, if you could use these results to increase organic purchases by even a percentage point or two, that would be worth doing – so this is an example where even an apparently low fit statistic may still have value.

We'll discuss more about how regression relates to predictive analytics and to some examples from earlier chapters. But for now, the main point is that correlations between variables, including specific outcomes, can be used to help predict those outcomes and/or what marketing initiatives might be used to obtain those outcomes. When analyzing big data sets such as these, this path to prediction can be very powerful.

PREDICTIVE ANALYTICS: DECISION TREES

Regression is not the only tool that can be used for predictive analytics. A second option is decision tree analysis, but of a different type from that which some of you may have covered in a class such as operations management. The process is similar but rather than plotting out decisions and implications in order to organize a cost/benefit analysis of decision options, the tool is used to cut data in order to better predict outcomes. That may not make a lot of immediate sense to you, but a number of students find decision trees more intuitively appealing than regression in understanding how predictive analytics is done. The software and math behind it are again fairly complex but the procedures and concepts are straightforward.

Essentially, the process starts with some variable we want to predict; some set of possible outcomes. So, purchase/don't purchase, respond to promotion/don't respond, prefer webpage A/prefer webpage B, and similar choices or behaviors. The tree then builds by examining possible explanatory variables. It evaluates how each variable can be used to split the response variable, successfully predicting the specific outcomes. So, say we have a yes/no response variable, perhaps whether individuals in the database are loyalty club members. Assume it is split 50:50, with half the outcomes "yes" and half "no". Picking a specific observation or individual from the dataset, we would have a 50:50 shot at predicting whether the outcome was yes or no.

We may want to add another variable to the analysis, perhaps age. The software will compare the variable with the response variable and determine whether it can increase our prediction success. Further, it will discover the best place to split that independent variable in order to maximize prediction success. For example, it might run through all the options with the age variable and determine that splitting it at 39 years of age is optimal. For those under 39, 44 percent are loyalty club members and 56 percent are not. For those 39 and above, 55 percent are members, 45 percent are not. So if we have that piece of data on any particular individual within the database, we can substantially increase our likelihood of success at predicting whether they are loyalty members. Rather than a blind 50 percent chance, if we know the individual is 25, we would predict they are not a loyalty club member with a 56 percent probability of being correct. Similarly, for any new individual coming into the database, we can better predict whether they are likely to join the loyalty program. Whatever variable best improves predictive success, split at the point where dividing it best improves predictive success, that will be used to split the branches on the decision tree.

Adding more variables allows more cuts to the data. The point is to keep adding variables and keep cutting so as to drive up the probabilities of being correct on predictions. The software is pretty savvy in this regard, only adding variables that help, while dismissing those that don't (much like regression shows significant and not so significant independent variables). It can also divide into more than two groups and/or reuse a variable, as appropriate. In the above example, the first cut may have been by age, at 39. The next cut may have to do with marital status, improving prediction accuracy in all branches of the "tree". The next cut may come from age again. So the over-39 branch is divided into married, single, widowed/ divorced sub-branches. The over-39, married branch might then be cut again into < 28 and 28–39 sub-branches. If one of the "leaves" that results (e.g. married, 28–39) can get the prediction success rate higher (60 percent, 70 percent, even higher), then we start to have something. The data analyst would continue playing with different variable and different cuts until they feel they have maximized the predictive capabilities of the data using this approach.

Decision tree analysis in SAS Visual Analytics starts with a new exploration. You can use the same data set as in the previous section, which provides a chance to compare the two methods and some insight as to why you might prefer one or the other. So load the ORGANICS_VISTAT data. Choose the decision tree visualization, it's just to the left of the linear regression tile at the top. Drag in the variable we're trying to predict, "Organics Purchase". The software should automatically drop it in the "Response" space under the Roles tab on the right. If not, move it there. As you can see, we have just under 1.7 million observations. Of these, 1.27 million customers (75.23 percent) have not purchased organics, while roughly 400 000 customers (24.77 percent) have. Can we do a better job of predicting organics purchaser than just using these overall percentages?

From here, it's just a matter of dragging and dropping potential variables into the visualization. Any or all of the variables here has potential and since the process is so simple and optimizes itself, one would probably try all of them. For our purposes, let's try some that we might logically expect to have an impact. Drag "Gender", "Geographic Region", "Home Owner", "Loyalty Card Class", "Affluence Grade", "Age", "Loyalty Card Tenure", and "Recent 12 Month Purchases" into the visualization. You should see the decision tree take shape before you (it will shift as new variables are dropped in that might do a better job at predicting, either by themselves or in relation to the existing variables). Information is available on the tree itself, as you hover over branches/leaves or it is summarized in the colored horizontal bars you see underneath the tree. Note that blue corresponds to branches/leaves with majority organics purchasers, and green corresponds to those with majority organics non-purchasers (see Figure 7.4).

On the right, you can see, under the "Roles" tab, that the predictors Gender, Affluence Grade and Age are highlighted. This indicates they are being used in the tree. The rest of the variables, not highlighted, are not used. They are not of value in predicting organics purchase when applied to this decision tree.

To understand the tree structure, let's look at what's going on in the visualization. Starting at the top, you can see that the first cut is made by age. By hovering over the resulting branches, you can see that the cut is made at 42.4 years of age. Out of 1.224 million of that age or older, 83.9 percent do not buy organics. Of the 464 000 under 42.4, only 52.4 percent did not buy organics. So we see a substantial change in the predictive probabilities in just the first cut. From there, the pattern goes as follows:

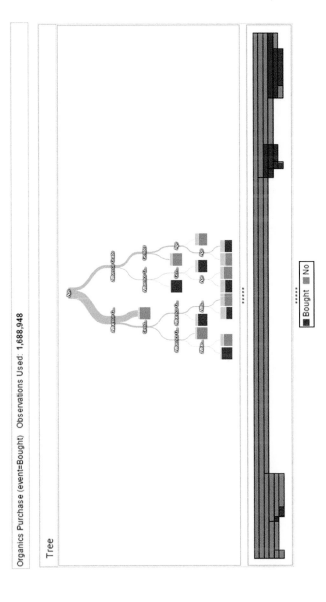

Figure 7.4   Decision tree example

- Age (≥42.4 years)
  - Affluence grade (≥10.2)
    - Gender (M,U)
      - Affluence grade (≥13.6)
      - Affluence grade (10.2–13.6)
    - Gender (F)
      - Affluence grade (13.6–18.7)
      - Affluence grade (≥18.7)
  - Affluence grade (<10.2)
- Age (<42.4 years)
  - Affluence grade (≥11.9)
    - Affluence grade (≥15.3)
    - Affluence grade (11.9–15.3)
      - Gender (M, U)
        - Age (21.05–42)
        - Age (<21.05)
      - Gender (F)
  - Affluence grade (<11.9)
    - Gender (M/U)
    - Gender (F)
      - Age (21.05–42.4)
        - Age (21.05–39.35)
        - Age (39.35–42.4)
      - Age (<21.05)

You can verify these results by hovering over the tree visual or, as noted, similar data come from the horizontal bars underneath. As you hover over those, you'll see a dot appear near the midpoint of each bar. Hovering over the dot will reveal the details of what's in each branch/leaf, not only the cuts made in predictor variables to get to that point but also the bought/no bought totals and percentages.

So that's the structure and process. And, again, with the variables it's given this will form the optimal predictor leaves, the segments of users that best predict specific responses. In this case, these are the segments with the highest percentage of users or non-users (high percentages of one or the other suggest less likelihood of making a mistaken prediction).

So, from a data analysis and marketing decision-making point of view, what can now be done with this output? One thing you should be able to notice right away is the color difference. As noted, green indicates majority non-purchasers while blue indicates majority purchasers or organics.

So if, from a marketing perspective, we want to identify the high-potential organics segment, we are interested in those colored blue. Further, you'll notice on the tree itself that the leaves colored blue or green are not always fully filled. Those closer to being filled illustrate the highest percentages of the behavior. So a full leaf of blue indicates the highest percentage of organics purchasers. Those close to empty show percentages closer to 50 percent. Finally, the size of the branch (you'll notice some are thicker than others) or, correspondingly, the width of the bar underneath is an indicator of the size of the leaf. So not only can we identify high percentages of desired behaviors but also segment size (100 percent of buyers means little if there are only five of them in the segment). Ideally, you want both a predisposition to purchase and a large segment having that predisposition.

So in continuing to process the results, we'd want to look at the indicated high potential segments. Those identified blue can reveal their statistics either from hovering over the leaf or finding the midpoint dot in the bars across the bottom. Moving from top to bottom and then left to right, the segments flagged by the analysis include:

1. 29000 total customers, $\geq$15.3 affluence grade, <42.4 years of age, 92.2% purchase organics (26904 customers);
2. 16720 total customers, $\geq$15.3 affluence grade, $\geq$42.4 years of age, female, 79.1% purchase organics (13224 customers);
3. 55784 total customers, 11.9–15.3 affluence grade, <42.4 years of age, female, 77.2% purchase organics (43016 customers);
4. 1824 total customers, $\geq$18.7 affluence grade, $\geq$42.4 years of age, male or unknown, 91.7% purchase organics (1672 customers);
5. 30000 total customers, 13.6–15.3 affluence grade, $\geq$42.4 years of age, female, 52.3% purchase organics (15884 customers);
6. 16340 total customers, 11.9–15.3 affluence grade, 21.05–42.4 years of age, male or unknown, 58.1% purchase organics (9500 customers);
7. 119320 total customers, <11.9 affluence grade, 21.05–39.35 years of age, female, 62.9% purchase organics (75012 customers).

From a marketing standpoint, this type of result can be very useful, but choice of segment may vary according to purpose. If one is looking for current organics purchasers (to introduce them to a new product, for a targeted promotion, or something similar), then those with highest customer counts would make sense, segment 7 followed by segment 3 and then segment 1. Alternatively, if you are looking for potential organics purchasers who fit the profile of current ones, you might prefer those with higher percentages, the 92 percent in segments 1 and 4 (though the very low totals in segment 4 might provide pause) followed by the 79 percent in segment 2 and 77 percent in segment 3. Or you may simply want to do some additional research into how and why they make organics decision purchases. If so, you've identified targets for additional, more in-depth studies.

All that supposes that you are making decisions and targeting according to segments. These kinds of results also allow individual identification and targeting. So if you find that some members of segment 3 are buying a newly introduced item at a high rate, you can target the rest of the segment with communications or offers. Similarly, if some members of segment 7 are responding to loyalty club offers at a higher rate, you can again increase that activity amongst those with similar profiles. As we'll discuss later in this chapter, this is exactly what some of the brands covered in this book do with their big data analytics, identifying and targeting customers based on what they know from their profiles.

Those sorts of initiatives are complex, involving potentially thousands of variables and millions of individuals. Think about all the items available at a grocery store or online retailer. Databases are capable of holding data not only about whether or not you and everyone else bought each item, but also on spending levels. So the data analytics can get to be a huge and incredibly complicated task. But this example does provide you with an idea of how it is done. When the data scientists provide you with appropriate results on such attitudes or behaviors, you can understand how they were generated and what they mean.

CLUSTERING ANALYSIS

A final related technique is clustering analysis. While this can be used for predictive analysis, it doesn't have to be. The main purpose is to group similar things together. These could be items purchased together (market basket analysis) or, once again, customer segments. Finding customer groups with similarities can also have potential, whether predictive or not. Understanding these types of associations can help with all marketing initiatives, including new product introductions, distribution decisions, predicting price sensitivity, or a whole range of marketing communication decisions (preferred media, acceptance of creative decisions, etc.). Or it can predict purchases if two or more items are commonly purchased together. The main point is to develop clear clusters that have similarities within but that are different across the groupings.

The approach with this tool is almost the opposite of decision trees though matters can end up in a similar place, with distinct segments identified. Where decision trees cut by variable values, slicing the data into ever smaller segments, clustering groups the similar outcomes of the variables. The effect is much the same but the emphasis is more on the similarities within the clusters than on the differences that separate them (though those arise as a by-product).

Clustering analysis starts with a set of observations defined by variables chosen for analysis. Note that the tool provided by SAS Visual Analytics only applies continuous variables ("measures") though one can transform a discrete/categorical variable into a continuous variable if necessary (using the log function, similar to what logistic regression does). We'll stick to the simpler case of continuous measures already available in the dataset.

Picture a group of observations laid out in two dimensions in a scatter plot. Clustering creates beginning "centroids". You can choose how many centroids (this determines how many clusters you end up with). The default within the SAS program is five. The software tool assigns each observation in the scatter plot to one of the centroids, the one closest to it. It calculates and sums all the distances between centroids and assigned observations. It then tries to move the centroids to reduce the distances, reassigning observations as they end up closer to a different centroid than their original connection. This iterative process continues until the software determines it can't reduce the summed up centroid/observation distances any further. The placement of the centroids is optimal to minimize the sum total of distances from observations to their closest centroids.

To see an example of the process and results, open the dataset BIGORGANICS. This is similar to the other organics purchase data we have been using; it just includes a few additional continuous variables we can use, as well as a categorical organics purchase variable that has already been converted to continuous form. You'll see six continuous measures on the left; drag and drop all of them except "Organics Count" into the visualization. Choose cluster analysis from the visualization tiles across the top (second one from the right). You should see the results as depicted in Figure 7.5: a series of two-dimensional graphs across the top and wavy lines across the bottom.

The top portion presents the results in the form we just discussed: identifying the centroids and then the surrounding observations assigned to each, by color. If you right-click on one of the graphs and choose "Explore",

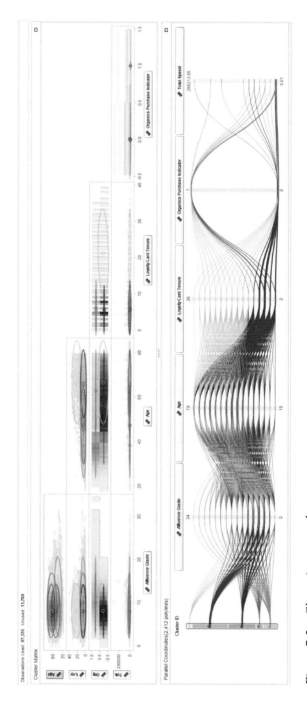

Figure 7.5   Clustering example

it will pop out for a better view. You'll notice a lot of overlap across the circles designating the assigned values but remember that the clustering and minimization of distances is done across six dimensions, not just these two. So it's possible that a smaller difference in one of these variables is countered by a bigger difference in one of the others. You'll also see that if you hover your mouse over the centroids, it tells you what the variable values are at that point. From the circles, you can get an idea of the spread of values around the centroid, whether there is wide or narrow dispersion.

The bottom half of the visualization also shows some of these results, identifying the clusters by color, once again, and showing how each color corresponds to each variable. The darker green cluster on the top, for example, can be followed by means of the "polylines" through each variable. If you click the darker green part of the "Cluster ID" column, you can isolate this one and its polylines. As you should be able to see, this cluster passes through lower values of the affluence variable, higher (though very spread out) through the age variable, also very spread out through the loyalty card tenure variable, a split result on organics purchase, and relatively low total spending, especially for those purchasing organics. This is what we're looking for with this visualization, a sense of what each cluster is like in terms of descriptors, attitudes, behaviors or other variables.

One can obtain hard numbers for each cluster. It's a little involved, but going back to the two-dimensional graphs above will get you there. As you right-click on each graph, it gives you the option to plot the specifics of each cluster by the two variables of that graph. You just have to go through the appropriate graphs to get all the variables (all the ones in a single row or a single column will do it for you). The result is a box plot of the variable values, by cluster (identified as clusters 0, 1, 2, 3, 4). The values given include the mean and dispersion measures like standard deviation and range. Just hover over each box plot to obtain the actual values. You should see the values shown in Table 7.2.

What do we have here? There are five distinct clusters. Initially, we have two younger clusters (0 and 3), one with a noticeably higher affluence grade and higher spending. These clusters are similar in terms of loyalty tenure but differ markedly in their likelihood to purchase organics. These are also relatively large clusters. The three older clusters (1, 2 and 4) have similar affluence grades and tend not to buy many organics (though there are some in clusters 1 and 4 who tried them). One of the clusters includes those with significantly higher loyalty tenure (cluster 1). Another spends considerably more than the others (cluster 4). Cluster 2 is non-descript in

Table 7.2   Cluster analysis results

	Cluster 0 (Blue)	Cluster 1 (Light Green)	Cluster 2 (Red)	Cluster 3 (Yellow)	Cluster 4 (Dark Green)
Size	21995	5040	31515	33810	4995
Affluence Grade	11.1	8.1	7.9	8.0	8.3
Age	45.1	66.6	65.4	45.6	63.6
Loyalty Tenure (months)	5.6	21.1	5.8	5.7	6.1
Organics Purchase (Y = 1, N = 0)	1.0	0.14	0.02	0	0.11
Total Spend ($)	2480.0	6383.9	4615.2	1983.0	27104.2

all areas, probably something of an average older shopper segment, especially given its size.

As noted at the start of this section, clustering can be used for predictive analysis. All one has to do is include a likelihood variable, whether purchase, promotional response, click-through, app download/use, or anything else in which you might have an interest. In this case, for example, we now have a pretty good idea who core organics buyers are: everything in the description of cluster 0. We could flesh out this description with additional variables and/or do some deeper analysis to see if we can find something out about the organics purchasers in clusters 1 and 4, allowing us to develop plans to target them.

The real value in clustering, however, is the deep descriptions and understanding of the different segments. If you've ever seen Nielsen's Claritas PRIZM segmentation product, you can get an idea of how such clustering can be of use. PRIZM combines zip code location with demographics and lifestyle data, including media and purchasing tendencies (e.g. favorite TV show, what kind of car they drive). The result is 66 segments across the US that clients can specifically target. If you can identify particular PRIZM clusters that buy your products, Nielsen can tell you more about them, help you find them, and suggest appropriate distribution and communication tactics to reach them. Similarly, if you are targeting a specific geographic location, PRIZM can identify the characteristics of major clusters living there and, again, all appropriate details concerning them. Clusters can be valuable in and of themselves, just for understanding target segments, whether used as a predictive tool or not.

WHAT TO USE?

Different means to similar ends; how do analysts choose the best tool? If using them to predict, the software actually provides a means to compare models. The final visualization on the right, the last tile, is named "Model Comparison" and looks for which model predicts best across the full range of variables. One of the items assessed in such situations is termed "lift". Lift is simply how much better we can predict when using the model than when not. If, for example, simple data show that 64 percent of respondents click through a current version of a website, we have a baseline. If we add a group of variables (demographics, lifestyle, etc.) that shows 74 percent click through, we have lift of 74 − 64 = 10 percent. If the click through was 56 percent, that may look good, in general, but since we know the baseline, it actually shows a loss in lift, 56 − 64 = −8 percent.

But even beyond testing the models for accuracy, they also provide different types of results. The regression approach works well when there is a linear relationship, when the correlation is consistently increasing, decreasing or staying constant. There are advanced techniques that can handle more complicated correlations (e.g. demand for a product is high when young, moderates in middle age, then goes up high again when older), but those add considerable complexity to the approach.

What regression does offer, however, are the specifics of the relationship. We know not only that the variables are correlated but also the magnitude and strength of that relationship. The results not only give us the independent variables but also how they influence the dependent variable (from the slope coefficient) and their relative importance (t-statistic). More advanced techniques can unravel whether the independent variables are correlated with each other (can be a problem) and provide solutions such as creating new, combination variables incorporating multiple independent ones (e.g. affluence might be a combination of income, wealth and occupation, all of which might be interrelated). For mathematical depth and insights, regression is quite valuable.

Predicting with decision trees is less about variable correlation and more about identifying, as precisely as possible, segments of interest. In the end, the segments are indeed correlated with some outcome, but only as a combination of independent variables, not specifying individual relationships that any of those independent variables have with the predicted outcome. This approach is probably best for identifying precise segments with high probabilities of some action or behavior. Ideally, a good decision tree would be able to isolate segments with very high probabilities of an outcome (e.g. >90 percent chance of responding to a promotional offer) that can be contrasted with segments with very high probabilities of the opposite (e.g. <10 percent chance of responding to the offer). And, obviously, bigger is better in terms of desirable segments but this technique has the ability to get down to a micro-segmentation level, which can then also help predict the behaviors of new individuals added to the database.

Clustering can do some very similar things when used for prediction though it's often used more for broader segmentation. Although advanced processes can go further, you may have noticed the default setting on the software was only for five clusters, quite different from the fifteen or so we obtained from decision trees. And adding more variables to the latter could significantly expand those numbers, while clustering would stick with the specified number of clusters. But clustering can do something that the predictive analytics can't, and that's create segments without a specific outcome or dependent variable in mind. Trying to identify and organize segments of interest without a specific product or communication outcome in mind is a larger task for many marketers, especially those trying to understand their customers better. Understanding moves into new product categories or new distribution channels may require a different sort of segmentation, more about gathering background demographics, lifestyle or behavior data on groups than on predicting a specific reaction to a specific initiative. That being said, the ability to then make predictions with such segments can be useful as well. And, as also mentioned, the depth of learning that can be obtained from cluster analysis is an excellent start to even further collection of data describing these segments.

The distinctions, including strengths and weaknesses of the different tools, can be more clearly seen in some specific, familiar examples. So we'll again turn to some of the extended applications from earlier chapters to show how these tools might have delivered those results.

RELATING BACK

As in the previous chapter, we can again illustrate where and how some of these tools are used by referencing real world examples. These cases also help clarify some of the differences in approach.

Regression

Recall the "First Five Seconds" testing that YouTube's unskippable labs does. As you might remember from that example, the group tests online video advertising, trying to judge how likely it is that a new ad will be viewed all the way through. Based on its analysis, the lab has collected variables representing 16 countries, 11 content areas and 170 creative aspects. Pairing these variables with other Google metrics, it can also add observations like brand recall and brand awareness. Doing the basic calculation, that's almost two hundred variables across the different categories subject to manipulation. These can include things like tone (humor, fear, rational appeals), visuals (expressions on faces, brand images), music (numerous options), and so on and so forth. Many of these will be categorical variables (a celebrity is in the ad or not), some may be scaled (degree of rationality), and others may be ratio data (time on screen, number of brand mentions).

For a database this big and trying to assess skippability, regression is tailor-made for the task. The point is not to judge an individual ad – we'll talk about that shortly. But in constructing the system for predicting that new ad, regression is the foundation. In this case, the dependent (y) variables would be length of time viewing the advertising, a continuous variable so standard linear regression could be used. All of the creative variables could be added as independent (x) variables, some discrete and some continuous. The country variables could also be added/tested, as could the content variables. Although the variables could conceivably be run all at once, the analysts would probably pick and choose variations, working towards identifying the more limited number of variables that have a correlation with viewing timespan.

Note that the categorical variables such as country or content would generate different equations for different values. So the creative values associated with an ad when viewed in the US might be different from the creative values found in Brazil. The intercept and slope coefficients would be different, as would the t-values. Variables shown to be significant in the US might not be significant in Brazil, and vice versa. Note also that the analysts could change the dependent variable. If the client wants to know the best version of the ad to increase brand awareness, along with viewing timespan, that could be done. In short, the regression equations developed from the online advertising big data establish key variables correlated with longer viewing times and other important marketing metrics.

The actual experimentation done on a new ad uses this framework, but doesn't necessarily require further regression analysis. The aspects of the new advertising corresponding to the testing framework (e.g. sexual appeal, electronic music, animation, brand logo on product) would be inserted into the regression equation. If several versions of the ad are under consideration or it is still not finished, each combination of variables would be inserted. From the results, the decision-maker can decide whether to go forward with the ad. From there, additional ad testing might actually be done. The final version or last few versions of the ad might be sent out as an additional test/experiment. But the framework constructed from regression would have already done its job in paring down the options.

Another illustrative case is music service Pandora. Pandora's methodology hasn't been discussed in this text but is an interesting contrast to Spotify's, which we did cover in an earlier chapter. We'll also talk a bit more about Spotify shortly.

Both music services stream music. With Spotify, users can choose their own songs to play though the service will try to predict other music they might like with tailored playlists or other recommendations for new music. Pandora, on the other hand, asks users to construct stations by seeding them with specific artists or songs they like. Pandora then chooses additional music that plays on the station based on its perception of user preferences – the user does not pick specific artists or songs but does have the power to like or dislike suggestions (the premium service does now allow user choice). So the services are somewhat similar on the surface but the algorithms and analytics behind them are quite different.

Pandora is based on a patented system it refers to as the Music Genome Project (MGP). The idea is that much like living organisms made up of differences in genes, so all songs are made up of distinctive characteristics that can be identified and catalogued. The MGP has hundreds of attributes, everything from vocalist gender to use of harmonies, heavy guitar to whether distortion is used, all the way to how funky the groove might be. All of the millions of songs in the catalog are classified by these attributes. All of the millions of users are also identified and have their background demographics and context data (where, when and how listened to).

From this huge database, Pandora can construct its stations. Certain songs show a strong correlation with a number of MGP attributes as well as user characteristics. If another song comes along with those same attributes, the algorithm will recommend it for that station that appeals to certain types of listeners in certain circumstances. The correlation, of course, is likely to come from some sort of advanced regression analysis. The prediction/ outcome is probability of liking a song. The independent song and listener characteristics correlated with that outcome are determined for each piece of music. Songs with similar significant independent variables predicting likability would be identified and included in similar stations.

While initial processing and recommendations would be based on segments with similar tastes and background to a new user, predicting their song preferences from the initial seeds, eventually the system can individualize predictions as well. Once enough observations have been gathered from an individual, there is a predictor specifically for them (their probability of liking a song). Other songs with similar characteristics will be recommended individually for them, even varying by context.

What both of these examples have in common is creating predictions from component pieces. Components of ads or components of songs, both can be combined with segment (or even personal) characteristics used in regression for predictive analytics. This is a strength of using regression. Not only can the critical components and characteristics be identified, but the relative strength of their contribution to the prediction can be assessed. The overall predictive power can be assessed. Even huge databases including all different kinds of variables can be inserted into some type of regression, generating sometimes invaluable results. Again, a caution. Regression has a wealth of variations and complications well beyond this text. We've only defined a few basic concepts, so use your knowledge of regression with care.

Decision Trees

Decision trees are also used for predictive analytics. We again have a result we want to accomplish and a bunch of variables that might be related to the preferred outcome. The technique cuts the data into ever smaller segments until we find the ones with the highest probability/association with the outcome.

Very early in this book and again in Chapter 4, we talked about loyalty programs in some detail. In particular, those at Caesar's. While experimenting with each individual customer is possible, it could be time-consuming if the firm needed to start from scratch with each new target. In determining what offers to make to loyalty members or other identified individuals,

Caesar's can fall back on what it already knows from its current massive database. Decision trees might be one way to accomplish that.

As we know, the database holds background information on individuals as well as records of activities, including locations, gaming activity and other attractions (resort/hotel rooms, restaurants, live shows). Gaming activities, in particular, can be more carefully tracked, everything from play metrics (machines or tables used, how long, amount won/lost) to environment (alone or group/family, lines, time spent onsite, other services like drinks or valet parking).

In order to develop an overall game plan for marketing offerings to loyalty members or others, Caesar's would designate an outcome it wants to predict. A positive response to a free room offer, for example. From the full database, variables could be brought in to divide members by probability of accepting the offer. Successive cuts would be made. So plays blackjack/doesn't play blackjack might be the first cut, followed by visits with spouse/visits alone. Then it might be a variable like age or takes in a show, or doesn't drink while playing. Each continues until some optimal segments are identified that would respond to the offer. Again, this would be the method to develop the algorithms for responses to loyalty members or registered users in general. If a new loyalty member shows up, from their profile you can see what that segment tends to respond to, given the decision tree results. That may need to be adjusted to the individual, but at least marketers aren't starting blind as to the type of relationship to which the target might respond.

Shopkick is another example of where decision trees could have been employed in order to create their business model. If you recall that case, Shopkick and other shopping apps are able to identify consumers when they are physically within stores, even pinpointed to specific aisle locations. Much like other loyalty programs, they are then able to communicate with the member, attracting attention to products and offering them information, discounts, or other promotional deals. What they and their retail clients want to predict is which outreach to the customer generates the most profitable response. If the individual is standing in front of the cereal selection, what information or offer will encourage them to pick a particular brand?

Once again, the database is filled with different variables about buying decisions, buying context, and shopper demographics, perhaps supplemented with additional background information on the consumers. In the full database, there is once again considerable data on what communications or offers have been successful, paired with all the other data. So a decision tree format focused on a specific outcome would yield exactly the type of results sought by retailers or their manufacturing partners. The result variables would be positive/negative response to a particular outreach: an informational ad for one of the brands, a price discount, a dollars-off coupon, buy-one-get-one, or any other type of promotion. To predict that outcome, the retailers would have a considerable array of variables to insert into the decision tree.

Initially, there are market basket variables, the buying patterns of virtually all the items in the store. A promotional offer on cheese may appeal to someone who buys crackers. There are the context variables including store location, time of day, frequency of visits, and so forth. And there are the individual demographics. If the customer has reported background information when signing up for Shopkick or another shopping app, that sort of data is available. If the customer can then also be matched with a credit card or other identifier, considerably more personal demographics and lifestyle data can be applied.

For the decision tree, then, an analyst would set the result variable (e.g. responds positively to a $1.00 off artisanal cheese offer), then pull any and all of the potential variables to be cut into the program. The tree would be constructed in a series of optimal cuts, anything from age or gender to other market basket items (e.g. gourmet crackers) to responses to previous offers or store location (perhaps in an affluent area). At the end, a few leaves/segments could be identified that have the highest probability of acting on the dollar-off promotion for artisanal cheese. And some segments would be identified as having very low probabilities, suggesting that they should not receive the offer, some other communication being more appropriate.

As noted in the previous example, what this process establishes is a structure for making offers, essentially an algorithm for who to approach. When a new individual is added, then, there is already some idea of what may appeal to them based on others who fit the same profile (segment). Based on their market baskets and reactions to communications/offers, the approaches can be further customized. But a decision tree would provide the initial guidance for how to approach them and similar shoppers.

So decision trees are also useful for predictive analytics but somewhat different from regression. Either could be used in a lot of situations, but you should be able to see that decision trees are particularly useful when identifying precise segments reflecting the sorting of lots of variables. When done, those specific segments are associated with desired outcomes, with precise probabilities on response likelihood. The exact relationship of each variable with the outcome can't be calculated, as is the case with regression. But in terms of identifying pertinent segments or other groupings by key variables (and eliminating non-key variables from consideration), the tool can be very useful for the appropriate applications.

Cluster Analysis

Finally, cluster analysis also groups variable outcomes into segments or other clusters. As noted earlier, these can be predictive if a result is one of the clustered outcomes. But clustering can be useful even without prediction applications. Where cluster analysis often makes a uniquely valuable contribution is in finding interesting segments. These segments may be associated not only with a current outcome of interest but as a marketing target for a number of other applications. So the strength of a prediction may be important but so may the potential for a valuable segment in any number of future marketing initiatives.

One common application of clustering is market basket analysis. What people buy on a shopping trip differs. My market basket is likely to look different from your market basket. But those groups of products do have patterns as well, and by clustering similarities in market baskets we are identifying similarities in purchase behavior among customers. That could lead to predictions or insights into the segment. When we discussed the Target pregnancy indicator, with the list of products that when purchased together indicated early stages of expecting, that was a form of market basket analysis. It's quite possible that was done with cluster analysis or something close to it.

Spotify is an example of a clustering approach. Pandora's Music Genome Project was detailed earlier as an example of using song characteristics to predict listener preferences. Spotify does much the same thing, predicting listening preferences, but does so in a different manner. As noted in our earlier discussion, Spotify collects some background data on subscribers as well as context data (where they listen to music, when, on what kind of device, etc.). But the core of their offering is tracking the music selections that listeners make. Out of the tens of millions of songs in its database, Spotify can track those to which any individual listens and those they don't. Listening preferences can be tracked by general categories such as genre, more specifically by artist, and even more specifically by song.

The example we used to demonstrate cluster analysis only identified five clusters and only used five variables. But, in fact, this type of analytics can be done with the massive number of variables (again, tens of millions of songs that listeners can potentially choose) in an application like Spotify and the numerous micro-segments that can be identified. What the software would do is group together listeners with similar preferences. If an identifiable group likes artists A, B and C while another likes artists X, Y and Z, those would be sorted into different clusters. Other identifying variables from demographics, lifestyle and context might also be added to the segment description. That can lead to their recommendations. If 80 percent of the ABC segment also listens to artist D or song MM, then it would make sense to recommend that choice to the other 20 percent as well. If an artist appealing to a specific micro-segment releases a new offering, it would be natural to target that cluster with the news. Similarly, if a new listener signs up, and that listener has a similar background and their initial music selections track an identifiable cluster, then recommendations would flow naturally.

The point is not similarities between facets of the songs but similarities between the listeners. Regression could probably get there as well, but clustering makes it easy to understand the approach of Spotify and how it differs from Pandora.

Another case we looked at that could apply cluster analysis would be Starbucks' Pumpkin Spice Latte (PSL). As noted in that example, Starbucks has accumulated extensive background data on PSL fans, often because they are registered for Starbucks Rewards. This can be combined with other demographics and lifestyle data once they have been identified, from other sources. Further, the PSL social media campaign has allowed further data to be collected, particularly when the digital fans can be matched to the other identifiers. Finally, for each individual, all interactions with Starbucks can then be tracked, from locations to purchases to preferred payment methods.

In this case, there is not necessarily an immediate behavior or outcome that Starbucks would want to predict. The PSL is already very popular with these consumers; they eagerly await its reintroduction every year. Marketing initiatives might be used to increase frequency of purchase or bundling with other products, which could serve a prediction purpose. But a more interesting application might be just to study this segment of users for deeper insights. A clustering analysis could be done, first to isolate this particular segment and to determine why they are different from other Starbucks customers. On a deeper level, there may also be sub-segments of interest. All PSL buyers may not be similar.

But once we've clustered the customer base, teasing out the PSL segment(s) by whatever descriptors (demographic, lifestyle, behavioral/usage), decision-makers could take a deeper look at them. By studying this segment and what their purchase drivers might be, Starbucks could develop a better understanding of how to introduce new products, how to better manage other specialty offerings, and/or how to develop enthusiastic digital media communities around its brands. The PSL cluster is unusually loyal and enthusiastic. Marketers should want to understand those types of clusters more deeply to inform actions aimed at them and at other segments. Cluster analysis makes that possible by objectively identifying the key variables separating the PSL segment(s) from the entire Starbuck customer universe.

So, as noted earlier, cluster analysis is particularly good at grouping things with similarities, distinguishing one group from another that is not so similar. Moreover, it identifies the key variables that dictate the clustering patterns. If a predictor is included as part of the clustering, it can be used for predictive analytics. But the unique contribution of using cluster analysis is the grouping and understanding of shopping goods, songs, customers or some other item of interest to marketers.

Index